Hope and Courage

Military Writers Society of America

2015 Anthology

RED ENGINE PRESS
Pittsburgh

Copyright: 2015 Military Writers Society of America

All Rights Reserved. No part of this book may be reproduced or transmitted in any form or by any means, electronic or mechanical, including photocopying, recording, or by an information storage and retrieval system (except by a reviewer who may quote brief passages in a review to be printed in a magazine, newspaper or on the Internet) without permission in writing from the publisher.

Library of Congress Control Number: 2015950538
ISBN: 978-1-943267-04-0

Red Engine Press
Bridgeville, PA 15017

Compiled and edited by Betsy Beard
Copyedited by Joyce Gilmour
Cover design and layout by Joyce Faulkner

World War II sketch by Howard Brodie
Courtesy of the Library of Congress

Printed in the United States

Writing for Healing,

Education,

Preservation of History

INTRODUCTION

Military Writers Society of America
Preserving History One Story at a Time

Have you ever wondered what it's like to be pinned down on a battlefield by withering mortar fire? Or pilot an out-of-control aircraft that has lost an engine? Or caught in a blazing inferno amidships? In the pages that follow you will find stories detailing exactly those types of scenarios, written by the men and women who experienced them. You will also find stories of humor and good cheer, stories of heartache and suffering, stories of things completely unrelated to military life, and historical accounts of events ranging from our country's inception to our current global conflicts. In short, within these pages there is something for everyone.

Each year, Military Writers Society of America (MWSA) publishes an anthology of stories, poems, and other creative works by its members. Our members represent a cross section of military culture—from enlisted men and women to officers in every branch of service—as well as family members and supporters. Many MWSA members have fought in conflicts, ranging from World War II, the Korean War, and the Vietnam Conflict, to the present-day Global War on Terror. We have served on every habitable continent. Many have experienced the death of a family member or close friend killed in action. Still others have returned from duty with wounds of the body, mind, or heart. And many of our members have supported those who are irreparably injured.

Military Writers Society of America was created as a "home" for military-genre authors as well as providing a safe environment for veterans who want to explore and deal with issues related to war and post traumatic stress. Most of all it was designed to be a meeting place for service members, veterans, their families, and people who love America.

Many of our stories revolve around combat scenarios, while a good few relate events of everyday living, whether from the service member's viewpoint or the viewpoint of family and friends. Our stories range from fiction sub-genres to nonfiction, memoir to technical reporting. They can be about historical events that happened long before we lived and breathed, detailing events from the Revolutionary War, the Civil War, or other eras. Together they show military service in its many aspects: the good, the bad, and the ugly.

The stories herein are not exclusively about war, because military service is about so much more than combat. It's about training and discipline, protecting the freedoms Americans enjoy, and providing a deterrent to those who would harm us. It's about danger and tragedy, true, and it's also about humor and compassion. It's about faithfulness, loyalty, courage, and hope. You'll discover a little of each in the pages that follow.

Betsy Beard

Vice President, Military Writers Society of America
Author of *Klinger, A Story of Honor and Hope*
Mom of Army Spc. Bradley S. Beard, KIA October 14, 2004

CONTENTS

1

MOMENT OF HOPE

Bobby Hart

People who know I spent two years in the Iraqi theater often ask me what I think will happen now that the U.S. military has pulled out. I can always answer with certainty, "I don't know."

All of us who were here have questions. In 2003-2004, we drove in SUVs all over Iraq. We visited villages, ate with the locals, built schools, and left with a pretty good feeling that things were going to turn out all right.

Then when we returned just a couple of years later, we listened to constant shooting and bombs and reports about hundreds of attacks each day and the dozens of soldiers and hundreds of civilians who died every day. Now we hear reports of ISIS taking over cities that our troops liberated, and there appears to be no end in sight. I wish I could say things are going to turn out well, and there have been signs of progress, but when there is such deep-rooted hatred, you have to wonder.

When my battalion deployed to Bosnia back in 1995—a mission I missed due to someone volunteering to go in my place—my boss had a Bosnian soldier who served as an aide and interpreter.

On the last night our battalion was there, my boss asked this soldier if we had done any good. The man assured him we had. "This is the only period of relative peace we have known in many years," he said.

My boss asked what would happen when we left. "Before you came, soldiers came to my house, raped and killed my wife and killed my children," he said. "What would you do?"

I kind of get the same feeling about Iraq. These people have been killing each other for hundreds of years. Getting rid of one brutal dictator might help, but it won't change the hatred, just maybe shift the balance of power.

I questioned what good we did, but it took a young soldier to put things in perspective for me.

In the nineties, Seid Tanovic was a nine-year-old boy whose family was escaping the ethnic cleansing that was going on in Bosnia. As his family was leaving, armed men stopped their car and pulled his father and uncle from it. His mother, sobbing hysterically, drove away, and Seid sat in the backseat and watched his father being beaten in the street.

Seid's family moved to Chicago and he went to high school, became a citizen, and joined the Illinois National Guard. Upon graduation, he earned a full engineering scholarship to Dartmouth. After his junior year, he requested a leave of absence and volunteered to go to Iraq and drove convoys through the war zone. I asked him why he would do something like this after all he and his family had been through.

He said, "Sir, if me being here gives one Iraqi kid the same opportunity that America has given me, then this is where I have to be."

Every time I questioned why I was there, I remembered this young man and it made me feel better. But still I wasn't real optimistic about the future...until one of my last days in Iraq. And it was nothing anybody did that changed my mind.

I was waiting for some of my people, so I walked down and sat by a small lake. While I was there, I noticed something was strange. I wasn't sure what; I just felt something was different. Then it dawned on me: it was quiet. There were no sounds of explosions, gunfire, helicopters, generators, military vehicles, nothing—just quiet.

The sun was setting, sending rays of white light through the reddened skies and graceful vapor trails of the jets and planes as they performed combat landings at Baghdad International Airport. When I was a kid, I was convinced the rays of light passing through the clouds were God's way of watching us.

As I sat there, the ever-present pigeons and wrens were flying around looking for a handout. Then a dove—not a white dove unfortunately, but a dirty gray, pigeon-looking dove—landed in a tree next to me.

And suddenly, I had an incredible sense of peacefulness. I thought for the first time that despite all the ugliness, there is hope in this land. The dove and I sat there for a long time. As I stood up to leave, a helicopter flew over and the dove flew off. In the distance, I heard an explosion. Things were back to normal.

But at least for a moment, I had seen what could be.

Bobby Hart

Lieutenant Colonel Bobby Hart (retired) spent twenty-five years in the Army Reserves and National Guard, including two year-long deployments to Southwest Asia. Hart is the second in three generations of his family to receive the Bronze Star Medal. His father, PFC Robert Hart, landed at Normandy and received his in Europe, while his son, Major Dustin Hart, received the Bronze Star Medal for his service in Afghanistan.

Hart deployed to Iraq with the 143rd Transportation Command in 2003 and served as a battle captain and public affairs officer for that organization, which operated ports and ran convoys that were some of the longest in the history of war. He returned in 2006 with the Task Force 3 Medcom, which provided medical support (including four combat support hospitals) throughout Iraq and helped American troops survive their injuries at a rate higher than 95 percent, the highest wartime survival rate ever.

Hart taught in Florida public schools including the University of Florida, Florida Gateway College, and Florida State College. He has received numerous commendations for the military, coaching, and teaching, and was selected as the Veterans of Foreign War's Florida Citizen-Educator in 2009.

In 2013, Hart wrote *Karaoke Singing Camels?*, an award-winning book that details the sacrifices our men and women in uniform make to protect our freedom.

He and his wife Cheryl, also a lifelong educator, are both retired and live in the middle of the Osceola National Forest in Florida. They have two sons, three grandsons, and three granddaughters.

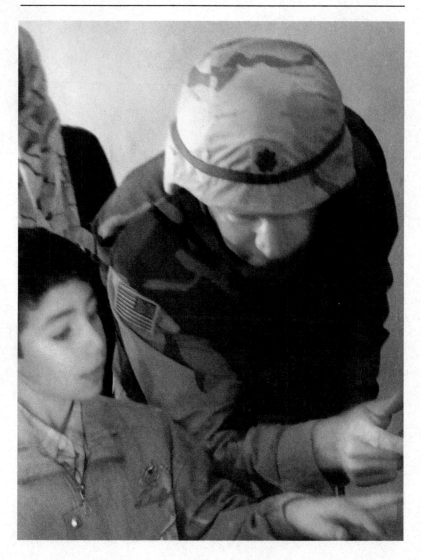

Soldiers help provide a better future for children in Al Nasiriyah
Photo by SGM Lawrence Stevens

2

STRAW HEAD'S BURDEN

James Lockhart

I led the battalion reconnaissance platoon, known as recon. Recon had an aura of mystery and danger. We were mysterious because others in the battalion didn't know exactly what we did. And although everyone in Vietnam was in danger, we were exposed to more peril due to the nature of our mission.

That mission was to seek out the enemy in remote areas and report his location to the battalion tactical operations center (TOC) without engaging him. Artillery, helicopter gunships, or Air Force fighters would then be deployed to attack the enemy. That was the theory. If we felt that we could directly engage the enemy, we would do so. This was always a gamble since we usually had as few as five men on a patrol.

In the jungle-covered mountains, there could be no reinforcements if we encountered and could not evade a superior force. Few clearings were available for medevac helicopters to pick up wounded. This was why there was more danger than mystery in recon.

A vivid memory I have involves a patrol with ten men in the mountains at the extreme range of supporting artillery. It started like most such patrols, but unsurprisingly evolved into a unique and transformative experience.

One soldier on that patrol was very pale, young, and thin; I think the word sallow described him best. Although we tried to recruit experienced people from the battalion's rifle companies for recon, many were reluctant to join us, perhaps due to the mystery—or the danger. This kid was newly arrived in Vietnam, had no combat experience, and was not a volunteer to recon. His short, thick, yellow hair stood straight up due to perpetual sweat. Thus he was known as Straw Head and would remain so until he could contrive a more pleasing nickname that everyone would accept. To make sure that Straw Head was tough enough for recon, I had given him the platoon's 25-pound radio to carry on this, his first operation.

For the first five days of the patrol, we had routine enemy sightings and one or two direct encounters with Viet Cong. Then I received an urgent radio message from the TOC in the late afternoon saying that we had to depart our location immediately and proceed eastward as fast as possible. Trying to move quickly while remaining undiscovered by the enemy was never a viable option and doing so in the impending darkness made it even worse.

Eventually it was revealed why this haste was necessary. A large B-52 bombing raid was scheduled for that night, dangerously near our location. My reaction was, "Why can't the bombing raid be canceled?" The TOC replied that such a request would have to travel up the chain of command all the way to General Westmorland's headquarters and then over to the Strategic Air Command. There just wasn't enough time. And anyway, the TOC would look like dummies for letting the patrol go out to that area when they knew a B-52 mission was scheduled there. The TOC didn't actually articulate this last statement.

My plan was to follow a 25-foot-deep dry riverbed that ran generally east. This ravine was easier to travel than going directly through the jungle undergrowth, so of course that meant the enemy might be using it also. We knew these deep valleys were ideal for VC encampments because they were relatively impervious to the nightly, random harassment and interdiction artillery rounds fired by U.S. forces. Using the wide trails on the crests of the ridges would have been much easier, but the enemy placed ambushes on them in the same way we did. An additional disadvantage in the riverbed was that, on the best day, determining your location on a map in such a constricted channel was difficult. At night, while trying to maintain light discipline, it approached the impossible.

There was also the issue of maintaining unit integrity in such a defile. It was a constant repetition of bumping blindly into the man in front and later realizing that he had moved on unnoticed in the dark. Noise discipline, one of our platoon's most cherished techniques, was impossible in a dry brush-ridden streambed at night.

At one point in the complete darkness, I froze as I'm sure every experienced man in the patrol did. Wafting from somewhere in the riverbed was the unmistakable aroma of ngoc mam, the universal Vietnamese fish sauce condiment. It could have only one meaning: VC were camping somewhere nearby.

From the moment darkness had fallen, I had tried to imagine what a firefight would be like in this confined space with a single file of men negotiating irregular terrain. It would be a nightmare to control the patrol with no visibility and deafening echoes of rifle fire in the narrow space. My only guess as to why we made it unmolested through that area was that the enemy was just as unsure of us and our strength as we were of theirs.

Every fifteen minutes the TOC was on the radio asking for our position. I was reluctant even to use a red-filtered flashlight to read my map, and that was assuming that I could have ascertained our location. I began to give our location as a reference to our last reported. "We've moved another 300 meters due east."

As time wore on and the time over target for the B-52s approached, the TOC became more demanding of our progress, and I began to add an extra fifty and then a hundred meters to our perceived location. I now strongly believe that the TOC as well as the intermediate headquarters did the same, so that at some point our actual position was at least 500 meters short of what was reported to higher headquarters.

Eventually, we had to stop. We were exhausted from a normal day of patrolling, and then we had endured this stressful surprise forced march. We found a ledge above the streambed and flopped down with little semblance of proper security. I doubt that anyone heard the earth-shaking explosions from the B-52 raid. I know I didn't.

And Straw Head? As my radio operator, he was one of the few men who knew the real situation minute by minute and the imminent peril we were in. He also bore a greater physical burden with the radio than any of us. As we neared our night location, from his position directly behind me in the file, I could hear him quietly weeping. The stress on him must have been tremendous.

On that patrol, Straw Head did not go to pieces, utter a single complaint, or commit any endangering blunders, as a rookie might have done. Even the most experienced of us had our nerves stretched by the uncertainty of the situation. Although I surely had overburdened him on his first patrol, he met the challenge with an unexpected and exceptionally deep reserve of strength. It did not require him to assault a machine-gun position or fall on a grenade to prove his courage, but he emerged from that patrol as a self-confident, respected member of recon.

His nickname remained Straw Head by his own choice.

James Lockhart

James Lockhart, originally from northwest Ohio, embarked in his late teens on the first of his three distinct careers. Joining the Army in 1961, he served with the Signal Corps in Korea, Maryland, and Japan. He rose quickly to the rank of sergeant before volunteering for Infantry Officers Candidate School. Upon his graduation as a second lieutenant, he reported to Vietnam in March 1968. There he led infantry units with increasing levels of responsibility, culminating in the command of an infantry company.

James completed Airborne and Special Forces schooling and returned to Vietnam in late 1970. He took an active and influential role in the Special Forces' training of Cambodian army infantry battalions for the next eighteen months. The remainder of his military career was spent in Special Forces as a commander, staff officer, and reserve component advisor. He retired from the Army in 1982.

In his second career, James parlayed his early Signal Corps training to join AT&T as a Technical Consultant and Account Executive. He later worked with AT&T alternate channel firms in technical and sales management.

His last career combined his teaching expertise from Special Forces with technical knowledge from AT&T as an associate professor and dean with DeVry University. In these roles he supervised faculty, developed laboratory manuals, counseled students, and taught a wide variety of courses in telecommunication and networking. He retired from DeVry after seventeen years.

Living in southern California, James is a drummer in a rock-and-roll band and writes traditional country music songs.

3

MY FATHER'S OFFICE

Candace George Thompson

When I was growing up, there was no Take Your Daughter to Work Day. I doubt I would have been interested anyway. There's nothing exciting about an office in a drab building on a military base where everyone wears the same uniform and sits at identical gray metal desks.

My father was an Air Force officer, a navigator and an orderly and precise man. His workspace would have looked the same whether in Okinawa, California, Alaska, Massachusetts, or any of the twenty-plus places he was stationed.

None of his terrestrial offices thrilled and inspired him the way his office in the sky did. Surrounded by instruments, dials, and levers, thousands of feet above the ground, he guided crews in B-24s, B-29s, B-52s, and RB-47s. Named Liberator, Superfortress, Stratofortress, and Stratojet, a cramped space in these giant birds was his workplace.

Despite my father's life-long love of airplanes and flying, I rarely heard him talk about his World War II experience until I asked him about it on his 81st birthday. He told me his first mission was in a B-24 on D-Day: June 5, 1944.

"We were awakened just after midnight and sent straight to the mess for breakfast," he recalled. "From there we went to the locker area where we suited up and headed to the briefing room. We didn't know anything about what the mission was."

Suiting up was no small task. B-24s weren't heated or pressurized—impossible because they didn't come close to being airtight. Frigid air rushed through the fuselage. Airmen wore woolen long-johns and electrically heated suits, over which they added sheepskin-lined coveralls and flak vests. A life jacket came next, and finally a parachute.

The flyers also wore electric gloves, wool caps, helmets, and oxygen masks. They needed headsets to communicate with crewmembers over the roar of the engines and the wind.

After my father broke his silence about his World War II experience, I became interested in the B-24, and four years after his death, I booked space on the only B-24 still flying.

I climbed into the plane and stood in my father's office—the navigator's cramped workspace behind the cockpit.

I knew I couldn't recreate a wartime experience on a thirty-minute low and slow flight over Chicago. I didn't need an oxygen mask. No lives would depend on my interpretation of instruments or celestial calculations. This B-24 would not be attacked by the flak of enemy fighters.

Nevertheless, I now have a vivid sense of my father's most memorable flight which occurred on July 29, 1944, the one for which he was awarded the Distinguished Flying Cross.

"The nearest we came to going down," he told me, "was on a mission near Bremen, Germany, to bomb an oil storage center. We were hit with three bursts of flak just before we dropped our bombs. We lost control of everything. The aileron was severed. The plane dropped about 6,000 feet. We couldn't get air speed to catch up with the formation.

"Our crew of ten had agreed months before that we would prefer to crash land or bail out over land, rather than risk certain death by ditching in the frigid North Sea. There was no good reason to think we could get back. We didn't have navigation; we didn't know if we had lost fuel. We were not air-worthy. I already had my parachute ready to go.

"Almost all at the same time, I heard the rest of the men shout, 'Let's go home!'"

At this point in his narration, my father began to sob. After composing himself he continued.

"With that, I settled down. I couldn't talk to the crew—my communication system was down. I was standing on the ammo can with one foot on either side and a hand on the astrodome for celestial observation. I tapped the pilot and co-pilot's feet with a yardstick and pointed to give them a course change.

"We headed for what I thought was the way to the ocean. I was just guessing; none of the four compasses were pointing in the same direction. England was some 300 miles away. The plane was listing to one side.

"When we got back to Seething—our base—we bailed out, all but three of the crew, and managed to make it to Wood-bridge, an auxiliary field with a long, wide runway where we somehow made a safe landing. One of our guys counted over 200 holes in the plane.

"And for that I was awarded the Distinguished Flying Cross," he concluded, and got choked up again.

*****

I've now seen the aileron control for banking and rolling—a fairly flimsy-looking exposed cable that the engineer on my flight warned us not to grab. I've stood where my father stood when they "lost control of everything."

Now I, too, have negotiated the narrow nine-inch-wide keel beam down the center of the bomb bay, albeit with the doors below it *closed*, to the large rectangular open hatches of the waist guns, as my father did on many missions.

I've experienced the roar of air rushing through the open plane, so loud it's impossible to hold a conversation. I've touched the aircraft's fragile aluminum skin, so easily punctured, no match for flak or machine-gun fire.

And now I have an even deeper respect—an informed, first hand respect—for my navigator father's skill and courage, and for all men and women who flew these early airplanes with primitive instruments, exposed to frostbite at temperatures as low as forty below, on flights that could last more than eight hours, all the while being attacked by enemy fire.

Sixty-seven years later, I finally visited my father's office.

B-24s in flight. Photo by Candace's father, Rex H. George, 1944.

Candace George Thompson

Candace George Thompson is the daughter of a career Air Force officer whose first mission was on D-Day. She was born in Kentucky, as were both her parents, and like most service families, hers moved frequently. By the time she started tenth grade, she had changed schools thirteen times.

Candace graduated from Antioch College with a bachelor's degree in Spanish literature and joined the Peace Corps as a volunteer to Venezuela. She earned a master's degree in organization effectiveness from Loyola University in Chicago.

Her first book, *Still Having Fun, a Portrait of the Military Marriage of Rex and Bettie George* is a romance, a history lesson, and a testament to the character and resilience of American military families. She is thrilled to report that the book was awarded first place in biography by Military Writers Society of America and won a bronze medal from Branson Stars and Flags.

Candace and her husband have now lived in Chicago for more than thirty-five years—eight times longer than any place before. She is happy to have finally found a home. Her interests include reading, writing, sharing a good meal with friends, laughing, early morning walks, rock 'n' roll, squirrels and penguins, Mexico, weird tidbits of information, and last but not least, her wonderful, supportive husband.

Candace's stories have been published in several anthologies including *The Heart of Christmas, Coast Lines 2, Overcoming,* and MWSA's 2012, 2013, and 2014 anthologies.

4

BIRD STRIKE

Brinn Colenda

The cluster of birds appeared out of nowhere, grew huge in the Plexiglas, and smashed through the windscreen at 200 knots, like feathered cannonballs. The pain in Lieutenant John Royal's body was incredible and instantaneous. He lost consciousness.

Texas wind swirled around the cockpit of the T-37 jet trainer, battering him with papers and loose objects. He could sense acceleration; G forces squashed him against the side of the cockpit. His left eyelid finally responded. All he could see was the ground spiraling beneath him. Odd. Where's the sky?

Oh my God, we're in a dive! He groped for the stick. Pain surged through his shoulder and right arm. Wings level, pull. Get the nose up! The ground hurtled toward him, airspeed increasing. Throttles idle. "Speed brake, speed brake!" he shouted into his mask. The pain in his shoulder screamed. He used both hands and pulled harder on the stick. The nose of the jet tracked upwards. God, this plane is heavy. He leveled off just before stalling the aircraft.

Royal was woozy, slow, like he had lost fifty IQ points. Air flooded into the cockpit like shrieking banshees.

What happened? Royal counted five, no, six fist-sized holes in the windscreen. His instructor, Captain Swinkels, seated alongside him, slumped against the opposite side of the cockpit, helmet and upper body splattered with feathers and what must be bird guts. His visors were smashed in, blood everywhere. Dead? Can't tell, but he sure looks bad.

Royal fought to keep the airplane level. Outside, the horizon stretched as far as he could see. A beautiful summer day, clear and serene. Inside, chaos. A fire hose of high-speed air rocked Swinkels and stabbed Royal in the shoulder like a steel rod.

Now what? Damn, my first ride. What do I know about flying a jet? His heart raced. Every movement sent shards of pain lancing through his body and the noise was horrendous. He longed to close his one good eye and slip back into the cocoon of blackness. So easy...

He jerked upright. Wake up, Johnny boy.

He took stock: he was a student pilot flying a wounded airplane that he had never been in before, his right shoulder was on fire, a possible concussion threatened to drag him back into darkness, something was wrong with one eye. Plus an unconscious instructor who may or may not be dead.

Great. Just great.

Okay, Johnny, by the numbers: maintain aircraft control, analyze the situation, take proper action. Slow this baby down.

The roar of the wind dropped with the decrease in speed. Better.

He checked his instruments. He guessed they were all normal and in the green. Fuel still okay. For the time being.

"Oh yeah, transponder." He groped around to find the dial and put in 7700, the code for emergencies. Dialing the proper numbers in the transponder cost him four hundred feet of altitude. "Johnny, you gotta do better than that."

"Where are we?" He tried to scan the horizon to pick out something familiar. "There's Wichita Falls...there's Lake Wichita. I know where that's supposed to be." His eye traced northwest to the flat areas where Sheppard Air Force Base sprawled across the Texas landscape. He dipped a wing. He could make out the runways.

Altimeter check: five thousand feet, more or less level.

He took a deep breath to calm his jumpy nerves before making his first radio call. "Bull Two Four on Guard. I need a frequency."

"Aircraft on Guard, contact Sheppard Approach on channel eight."

He switched the frequency. "Approach, this is Bull Two Four. I am declaring an emergency."

"Bull Two Four, state your emergency."

"Approach, we took a bird strike. My instructor is unconscious."

"Bull Two Four, stand by."

Stand by? What do they think this is, a simulator? I need help now.

"Bull Two Four, this is Colonel Tritten. How are you doing, Lieutenant?"

Colonel Tritten? What's the wing commander doing here? "Sir, I've had better days."

"Confirm that your instructor is not responsive."

"He's not moving. I can't tell how badly he's hurt."

Another pause.

"Bull Two Four, Approach will vector you to the bailout area. Then you will eject. That's an order, Lieutenant. Do you understand?"

Royal's head snapped back in surprise and he gasped in pain. His heart raced. Leave the captain? What if he's not dead?

"Bull Two Four, I've ejected myself. It's not that bad. Trust your equipment, son. It will save you. We don't want to lose you, too."

He thinks I'm scared. Well, he's right. Royal laughed. What he's trying to do is give me an excuse for abandoning the captain. He's covering my butt for me. Royal glanced over at Swinkels' inert form.

Maybe he's right. I've never landed anything heavier than a Cessna. Who am I kidding? I'm no Chuck Yeager.

The summer rough choppy air made him focus on flying. It was like driving on a road dimpled with potholes. He knew about uplift from his glider days at the academy. Somehow the familiarity made him feel better.

"Lieutenant, I say again, you will fly to the bailout area and eject."

I can't leave this guy. He's my instructor, for Christ's sake.

Royal punched the mic button. "Sir, I am now pilot-in-command and I'm bringing the captain home. I have the runway in sight. Going to RSU frequency. Bull Two Four Out."

Maintain aircraft control, he chanted. Jesus, I sound like a robot. He chuckled, then turned serious. Okay, Johnny boy, let's get this beauty on the ground. He gauged his rate of descent, cross-checked his altitude, and slowed down.

He called to the T-37 Runway Supervisory Unit that would direct his landing approach. "Cooter, this is Bull Two Four, about five miles northwest, three thousand feet descending. Request emergency straight-in approach."

"Bull Two Four, Cooter. You are cleared for a straight-in approach, runway One Five left. I'll read you the checklist. Do one item at a time. But fly the airplane first and foremost. Got that, Lieutenant? Acknowledge."

"Wilco."

"Bull Two Four, there will be a small pond on your left at two miles. Put your gear down there. We have you in sight. Just keep flying the airplane."

What pond? Where? Okay, there it is. Gear down. The aircraft wallowed and he felt the gear extending. Three green lights. Best news of the day. "Trim, Johnny, trim." He added power. "Airspeed, Johnny. Airspeed, attitude. Airspeed, attitude." The leather palms of his flying gloves were all greasy, whether from sweat or bird guts, who knew?

The concrete runway stretched out in front. All he had to do was to set the plane down, keep it on the runway, and stop. He banged down hard, bounced. Hold the attitude, Johnny. The plane bounced again. Stayed down.

Brakes! The plane abruptly swerved left. John overcorrected right, then swerved left again. Finally he stopped the plane and shut down the engines. Outside, pandemonium exploded as emergency crews rushed at him. Inside, blessed quiet.

He smiled as he closed his eyes and let himself slip back into unconsciousness. It had been one hell of a ride.

Brinn Colenda

Brinn Colenda is a graduate of the United State Air Force Academy and a retired lieutenant colonel. He served in a variety of flying and staff assignments around the world from Southeast Asia to Bolivia. He was an instructor pilot with the U.S. Air Force, the German Air Force, the Dutch Air Force, Great Britain's Royal Air Force, and was awarded command pilot wings by the Bolivian Air Force.

He has advanced degrees in economics and business, and had a postgraduate fellowship at the Hoover Institution on War, Revolution, and Peace at Stanford University.

Brinn has published articles in professional journals and his local newspaper. His first political-military thriller novel, *The Cochabamba Conspiracy,* won awards from the Military Writers Society of America and the SouthWest Writers Association. His second thriller, *Chita Quest,* explores MIA/POW issues as well as military families under stress. It won awards from the Florida Authors and Publishers Association and first place from the New Mexico-Arizona Book Cooperative. He is currently working on his third in the series, planned for release in autumn 2015.

Brinn serves on the Angel Fire Village Council and spends the rest of his time skiing and writing in the mountains of northern New Mexico with his wife and three college-age sons.

Brinn Colenda, Exchange Qualified Flying Instructor (QFI) with the Royal Air Force, 1980-1982

5

THINGS THAT GO BUMP IN THE NIGHT

Kristen Tsetsi

"I can't believe we have a gun," I said to my husband Ian. "Like, a real gun."

"I know," he said. He's in the military, so he has weapons experience—rifles, handguns, grenades, and things—but we'd never had any of those in the house.

Driving home with a new gun on the floor of the back seat, I recognized that gun ownership is a unique responsibility. I didn't want to buy it to "beat the government" in case they decided to "take our guns," nor am I a doomsday preparer, a gun fanatic, a militia member, or a drug dealer. However, I am, admittedly, someone who's seen too many true crime shows, with women as the victims ninety percent of the time. That seemed like a good reason to have a gun.

Before buying, we'd shot targets at the range for over an hour, and it had involved a lot of loading, unloading, spinning revolver cylinders, releasing magazines, pulling slides, and getting a few shell casings in the face right between the eyes, down the shirt, just above the glasses, in the hair. Ian couldn't figure out why they kept hitting me in the head when, any time he shot, they flew off somewhere over his shoulder. But even after all that, taking home my very own pistol and a box of bullets was an unexpectedly confusing experience.

I'm afraid of guns. Not in the "Eek! Gun!" way, but in the "I respect and am appropriately afraid of what they can do when fired" way. And after going to the range and shooting fairly well for a first-timer, I was interested in overcoming that fear. I wanted to be comfortable with guns and maintain a healthy respect with caution, rather than fear.

"I have to become one with the gun," I told Ian. I knew that was the only way I could go from "yeah, I know it's mine, but it still scares the crap out of me" to "yes, it's dangerous in the wrong hands, but I know how to use it, so it's fine."

And so I brought our new purchase inside, opened the padded case, and pulled out the 9mm. Its weight was surprising. Between the range and home, I'd forgotten how heavy it was. I expected plastic, maybe, like a squirt gun. I raised it and aimed and pulled the trigger. Nothing. Not even the click it makes when it isn't loaded (which, of course, it wasn't).

I tried to pull back the slide and wasn't strong enough. Stupid thing wouldn't budge. Everything had worked much better on the one we rented at the range. Probably something wrong with this one. What if it was defective? What if the first time I shot it, it backfired into my face like the gun used by the female assassin foiled by George Clooney in The American?

Ian, much stronger than I am, tried it himself. It was so tight everywhere that he looked it up online. "After firing about 300 rounds through it, it loosened up," someone wrote. Ian also found a lot of positive comments about the gun, in general, which was nice. Who doesn't like validation?

Hands aching, and frustrated by the no-worky, I aimed my new gun and pretended to pull the trigger a few times before putting it upstairs.

Then I hid the case in the coat closet so it wouldn't be seen if someone broke in. And then I hid the bullets. Just in case. When I saw some of the gun-purchase paperwork on the table, I hid that, too. What if someone walked by the window and peeked in and saw it?

What if, indeed. Someone was going to walk by my window, peer in, see the paperwork, and think, "Oh, awesome. They got a gun. I'm gonna break in and try to find it."?

Obviously, owning a deadly weapon was making me feel more paranoid than safe.

I had planned, and truly intended, to become familiar with the deadly weapon the next day, but on day two of ownership, I had to go to work. And then after work, you know, I was pretty tired.

On day three, it sat where it sat, in the place where I'd put it, the whole day and into that evening. After work, I was tired again, so it really wasn't the right time to...

"So!" Ian said that night at what seemed like a very late hour. (It was 1930.) "You want to take apart your gun?"

Why did everything have to be about the stupid gun? The gun I wanted to love but couldn't, because it had such bad potential. Not on its own, but in my hands. Everyone has moments when, say, they fall over for no reason, drop the same thing three times in a row, or accidentally wave a gun around in the range after being hit in the forehead with a shell-casing. (The bullets had all been expended with that one, so there was no danger. Luckily.)

That night, though, I just wasn't in the mood to learn anything. "What about tomorrow, right after work?" I said. "Oh, darn. Forgot. You're working late."

"Yep." He gave me a look. "You said you wanted to know it."

"Oh, fine."

Now, you may remember that everything on the gun was very tight. This made for a very frustrated Ian, the only one with the hand strength to (eventually) take off parts that relied on the movement of other parts that were absolutely not moving. Little by little, every moveable thing on the gun was slid, fiddled with, pulled, or pushed at least twenty times in the course of Ian's disassembly, and I watched all of it, learning along with him what steps to take. By the time he was done, I had it all in my head, and I told him I would do it myself the next day while he was at work.

"I'll send you pictures!" I told him.

On day four, I started carrying the gun everywhere with me. Maybe it was the disassembly, or maybe it was Ian's reminder to me about what I'd said I wanted to do. Whatever it was, my 9mm was now with me for coffee, walking through the house, sitting on the couch, and brushing my teeth.

After work, Ian's lesson still fresh in my head, I went through the disassembly process myself. And I experienced none of the trouble he did, thanks to all of his loosening. Putting it back together was just as uncomplicated, and Gun and I were friends. For a few hours, at least.

Later that night, things got a little weird. Ian was working late, so I carried the gun to the bedroom, where I watched some television (a crime show, which was probably a bad idea) before going to sleep.

But I'm a very light sleeper.

I'm also somewhat convinced I have bionic hearing. I used to work in someone's home office, and one day one of my boss's children was entertaining his siblings by blowing through a whistle that created sounds at various pitches. After a while, on one of the higher notes, I asked him if he'd consider doing that when I was done working.

"You can hear that?" he asked. "Only dogs are supposed to be able to hear that." (Make of that what you will.)

Thanks to my apparently dog-like hearing, a faint noise downstairs woke me up. I hadn't heard the garage door open and close (that would also have woken me up), so it couldn't be Ian. I looked at both my cats. They were still sleeping, so the noise must have been nothing.

I listened again, heard nothing, closed my eyes, and then heard it again, slightly louder. What the f*** is that? Still no movement from the cats. It wasn't someone walking around, or anything rhythmic. Just a single noise that was definitely in the house.

Before we brought Gun home, I had imagined what I'd do if someone broke in. It was simple: I'd reach for the gun, point it at the door, and wait. If someone (a stranger) came up the stairs, I'd shoot them. No problem. (For the sake of propriety or to avoid the risk of judgment, I feel like I should say, "I would first carefully consider the value of a human life and try very hard to wait until the last minute to shoot." However, it wouldn't be true. I do value life, but there are risks involved in breaking and entering, and most people know what they are.)

That night I didn't find myself reaching for the gun. Instead, I couldn't move. I've had noise-induced paralysis before, but this was different. I actually had the option to reach for a gun this time. And if I did that, it meant I was accepting the possibility of shooting someone. But imagining it now in a much more real way, it wasn't as simple, anymore. It was plain scary.

That aside, even if I were going to shoot someone, I'd have to slide in the magazine. When I'm downstairs, I can hear any movement upstairs. Someone else downstairs could probably do the same. If I so much as rolled over, they'd hear the shift in weight on the bed and possibly be encouraged to come up, and quickly.

Would I have time to reach for it, never mind load it? The magazine is loud when it slides in, and even louder is the click to lock it in. Could I roll over, grab the magazine, slide it in, take off the safety, and aim it in the time it would take someone to rush up the stairs?

The noise happened again, this time louder. A single bang/tap/click/something. I still couldn't move. Pickupthegunornot, pickupthegunornot, pickupthegunornot?

There's always a moment after hearing a strange noise when you tell yourself, "It's nothing. I know it's nothing. No one broke into my house." (Which is why the girls in scary movies always search the basement when they hear something down there. "Don't go!" the audience screams, but realistically, they'd all do the same thing. We never really think there's anything bad down there.)

The only way I would ever finally move—and start doing some regular breathing—would be to remind myself that a few weeks before I had decided to become a fearless person. So I reminded myself ("Fearless!") and forced myself out of bed.

I went downstairs to the living room with my phone gripped tight in my hand. At least with the phone, if I needed to run, I'd have it to call 9-1-1.

But there was no need to run or call.

It was just Ian, having a beer on the couch.

After I hugged him for being the cause of the noise, he said, "Why didn't you just call down and ask 'Who's there?'"

Final analysis: Not quite ready yet to use Gun in self-defense, but we're getting there.

Kristen Tsetsi

Kristen Tsetsi's father flew B-52s over Vietnam a few years before she was born. In 1981, when Kristen was seven years old, he was a federal civilian employee moving his two daughters to Headquarters USAREUR in Heidelberg, Germany, where they would stay into the 1990s. While attending high school in Heidelberg, Kristen played with writing but more seriously pursued a boy named Ian—a tall, mullet-haired, blue-eyed transfer with a dangling cross earring and a love of heavy metal. They dated for three weeks.

Ian left Germany after their 1992 high school graduation, and in 1993, Kristen's father's overseas position closed. This was the same year Ian mailed Kristen a shocking postcard that unfolded like an accordion to reveal a series of cartoon images of Army basic training.

Kristen avoided college for as long as possible after returning to the United States in 1994, but eventually earned her master's in creative writing, turning in stories often inspired by that boy from high school. Several appeared in print and online journals and her work went on to receive a Pushcart Prize nomination.

She proposed to Ian a year and a half after his 2004 return from Iraq with the 101st Airborne Division, a deployment that inspired Kristen's novel *Pretty Much True*, published—along with her second novel, *The Year of Dan Palace*—under the name Chris Jane.

Kristen and Ian live in Connecticut, where she writes and he is a major in the Connecticut Army National Guard.

6

A VISIT TO PARADISE

Hugh Aaron

The Philippines

World War II

There was one guy in our tent who was hard to figure. As I remember now, I guess I was the only one who figured he was hard to figure. The rest were damn sure he had a woman, which explained why he disappeared from camp every time we had a liberty. Sure, everybody disappeared from camp when they had liberty, but when they came back they talked about it. You knew where they went and what they did. The stories were always colorful because usually the guys got drunk and raised hell, and even if they did neither, they always said they did.

When this guy—his name was Fred—came back to camp after liberty, he never referred to where he'd been. Any time anyone would ask him, he'd laugh and say, "I've been out looking over the country." Once when he came back, one of the guys asked, "How was she?"

"Very nice, very nice," he'd answer and go back to reading. He read practically all the time. He didn't play cards with the rest of us. He didn't talk about women. He didn't knock the officers. He didn't gripe. He worked like a son of a gun no matter what he was working on, even digging ditches. We'd probably have hated him except that he minded his own business and was always congenial. Nobody gave him much thought. Only I did.

I was a kid then, about nineteen. I figured he was lonely, so I became his friend. But I didn't do this wholly on his account. I expected to get something out of it, maybe a new way of looking at things. For instance, he read books. I never read a book in my life. He had Shakespeare in his footlocker. I can remember seeing *War and Peace* and *Walden*. He had *The Magic Mountain*. Before I returned to the States I had even read it, my first book. And I've been reading ever since.

We never became close friends, but I didn't think he had a woman as the other guys thought. It didn't fit him. No, I figured he had something else going on when he left camp. He gave me the biggest clue a couple weeks before I found out what he was really doing. He got into an awful fight with Whitey.

Whitey, I should tell you, was a guy who was mixed up. That's the best way I can explain him. He never knew what he was doing and why he was doing it. He didn't care much about anything except getting back to the States. He raised more hell when he was on liberty than anybody in the battalion. We called him Whitey because of the color of his hair which was white as a poodle's. It hung down over his eyes like a poodle's, too. I used to wonder how a man could go through life seeing the world through hair.

He kept a still somewhere in the jungle, and fed the contraption pineapple and grapefruit juice which he stole from the commissary. No one could ever find it. Sometimes even he couldn't find it. Usually, though, he succeeded. Then already half lit he'd lie on his bunk, lift the can to his lips so that some of the liquid ran down behind his ears, and guzzle and gurgle like an ecstatic baby.

One afternoon, while he was doing exactly that, two Filipino girls visited to deliver our laundry. They were polite kids, quiet kids who did a good job for us, and we left them alone. Fred was lying in his bunk, reading as usual. I was sitting on mine, bent over a footlocker writing a letter. Two guys were playing poker at the table in the center of the tent. The girls came to me, gave me my stack of washed and ironed laundry, and I paid them. Then they went to Fred, who put down his book and paid them, saying "thank you" in English. Next they approached Whitey, but as soon as one of the girls got near enough, Whitey's arm shot out like a snake's tongue and grabbed the girl's arm. "Come in here with me," he said. He pulled her on top of him and tried to rip off her dress. The other girl went for Whitey and began beating him in the face. When the poker players saw her beating their buddy, they went for her, and pulled her away. It took both of them to do it.

I was sort of paralyzed, but Fred smashed his book to the floor and leapt to Whitey's bunk and pulled the first girl away from him. Whitey stood up looking stunned. Fred yelled something to the girls in their own language, and both girls fled.

"Why in hell did you do that?" Whitey demanded.

Fred didn't answer, and went back to his cot where he sat calming himself.

Whitey lay back in his bunk again. "When in hell we going to get out of this hellhole," he murmured.

Fred picked it up. "You've made it hell, Whitey. You've made paradise into hell," he said.

There were two things to notice about this incident which might have given me clues to where Fred went and what he was doing on liberty. One was his mention of paradise, and the other was his speaking the native tongue, very unusual for a GI since he couldn't have learned Tagalog anywhere but in the islands. At the time, I considered what he did for the girls more significant. Who knows what Whitey might have done? Fred did a courageous, noble thing. I told him what I thought, too.

"Well, they're just like friends everywhere."

"I would think so," I said.

"Except that they're warmer than we are, more accepting. We give our shirts, they give their hearts."

Then one thing led to another, and soon he was mentioning certain people by name, and the names of places, becoming more animated than I had ever seen him in the three years we'd been together.

"How'd you like to come with me on our next liberty?" he asked.

I was curious about where he was going, alright, so I said, "Sure, maybe it'll give me something to write home about."

Early on a Sunday morning, just as the sun was rising over the rim of the mountain range on the opposite side of the bay, Fred and I, carrying rucksacks on our shoulders, began our trip to somewhere inland. An Army truck picked us up and we sat in the back watching the countryside draw away behind us. The road was very straight and smooth.

"Nice road," I said.

"For us, yes, the way we're traveling," Fred said. "But not so good a few years ago for some other Americans. This is the road they walked in the Bataan Death March."

"No kidding," I said, "a nice concrete highway like this?" Somehow my words didn't come out right. I felt a little ashamed. Fred made no comment, for which I was grateful, and we traveled for some time before he spoke.

"See that tree, that mango tree there beside the house? An American from the march is buried beneath it."

"Yeah?" I said, very impressed. I asked myself, now how did he know that?

As if he heard, he answered, "Friend of mine buried him."

After a pause he added, "Died in her arms."

Her arms, her arms, her arms. The words kept repeating in my mind, because they caught me by surprise. I hadn't thought of a woman in connection with what he had been saying.

After we rode for an hour, he signaled the driver to let us off.

"What's out here?" the driver inquired. "You're in the middle of nowhere."

Fred laughed. "This is the place," he said.

Baffled, the driver zoomed off, leaving us standing at the entrance to a dirt road that was hardly more than a path. As we walked, Fred began going faster, and soon I had to run to keep up.

Some kids half-naked and some all the way, were running toward us, and as they drew near I heard them yelling "Fred, Fred. Americano. Comusta, Fred?" After they reached us they jumped all over him. He called them by their names and said something to them in Tagalog. They kept trying to get into his rucksack, so he stopped and opened it and gave each kid some gum and a candy bar. Waving their loot above their heads, they ran ahead of us shouting Fred's name.

In a few minutes we entered a small village of thatched huts on stilts. But there was no one around, only the kids.

"Where are the people?" I asked. Fred pointed to a small church at the end of the village street. Upon entering the church, we saw a hundred or so people seated on benches. The speaker on the dais stopped talking as the people all at once turned their heads toward us. From every direction I heard, "Psst. Psst." Everybody was inviting us to sit beside them.

The speaker, who I could tell had to be the clergyman, spoke perfect English without a trace of an accent. "For the benefit of our American visitors I shall continue my sermon in English."

A murmur spread throughout the room, and everybody nodded their heads, signifying they approved.

I didn't listen to the minister very closely. His speech was quite flowery. It was about his gratitude toward the Americans. With everyone staring at me, I was too uncomfortable to pay much attention to his every word. After the sermon, a plate was passed around. Fred dropped a couple of pesos into it, and I dropped an American half-dollar. What a stir that caused.

As the plate went around everyone looked at it as if they were collectors finding a rare coin. When the plate got back to the minister, he retrieved the coin and held it up for everyone to see.

Then he said to me, "Thank you, my friend. Can you tell me how much this is worth?"

"A...a peso, I think."

"That's right, Reverend," Fred said.

"May I, with your permission, replace it with a peso," the Reverend asked, "and retain it as a souvenir, a remembrance of your American generosity?"

Quite embarrassed, I nodded.

The people sang some church songs in their own language, ones that I also knew, only in English. The minister said a prayer, which ended the service. The people crowded around us, chatting with Fred, until the minister broke through and shook Fred's hand.

"You've had a long trip, and you need a cool drink. Come to my house, and you must introduce me to your friend."

Well, you'd think I was running for mayor. I must have shaken the hand of everybody in that village.

So I was right. Fred didn't have a woman. He had a whole village, because he loved them and they loved him. Now that I'm back in the States, I find myself thinking of Fred more than any of the other men I served with. I hope, now, that you'll think of him, too.

He was something, and so was the reverend, and so were his people.

[Excerpted from "A Visit to Paradise" in a short story collection currently under consideration for publication.]

Hugh Aaron

Hugh Aaron, born and raised in Worcester, Massachusetts, was educated in the Worcester Public Schools, and received a liberal arts degree in the humanities at The University of Chicago, where his professors encouraged him to pursue a literary career. However, he made his living as CEO of his own manufacturing business while continuing to write. Since he sold his business in 1984, he has devoted full time to his writing, resulting so far in two novels, a travel memoir, two short story collections, two collections of business essays, a book of movie reviews, three children's stories in verse, and a World War II letter collection. Several of the seventy short stories he has written have been published in national magazines. Eighteen essays on business management and one on World War II have appeared in the *Wall Street Journal.*

Hugh has written eleven full-length and sixteen one-act stage plays. His most recent books are a collection of five novellas entitled *Quintet* in 2005, a second collection of essays on business in 2009, and a second collection of short stories in 2010. Most of Hugh's plays deal with contemporary issues, several having had readings at local libraries, churches, and in private homes.

Hugh served three years in the Seabees during World War II, two of them in the Southwest Pacific. He lives with his artist wife in mid-coast Maine.

7

FEELINGS

Jerome Domask

April 10, 1990

Dear Dad,

These are thoughts I have never shared with you during the past years. Now I must speak. It is very painful, one of the most painful experiences of my life.

I wish I could share these feelings with you in person, but I'm concerned you would never understand at this stage in your life. You are almost ninety years old and the last thing I want to do at this time is take a chance of hurting you, when in fact I love you.

As a young boy I used to think you took me fishing just to row the boat, although many times we went river fishing. I can remember many days riding home from college with you, in silence. "What courses are you taking? What do you have planned for the weekend? What's going on in your life?" No questions. Only silence.

I learned during my sophomore year that you trusted me, loved me, and really cared. You came to my rescue when I was taken to the Waukesha Police Department on suspicion of hit and run. You told the officers I was telling the truth, I was innocent, and that I was being unjustly held. You demanded I be released immediately. It's probably one of the few times I can remember you raising your voice.

I returned from Vietnam and stopped to see you and Mom while passing through California to see Mary and the kids. I desperately wanted to share my experience of returning safely from Vietnam. I felt like a volcano ready to explode. I needed to talk! I will never forget Mom saying, "Don't be foolish." You remained silent.

These tears are beneficial. Just having you listen to me, and I know you are, helps me vent. It helps me to understand myself and in turn to relate to others. These feelings must be purged from my soul. I must work through this pain to go on learning and growing.

Some of the pain has receded. Several weeks ago, several days ago, several hours ago, I could not have written this letter. My future healing is based upon my ability to cry, to feel, to understand, so I may be in touch with my emotions. The shell of denial must be peeled back like an onion skin, one layer at a time, to begin to understand and to feel again.

Yesterday I could only speak and cry of the pain. Today I can write about it. Thank you for listening to me, Dad. It has been most helpful. The poisonous pedagogy in my mind can be broken. You are helping me by being a part of this dialogue. I love you, Dad! Thanks again.

Your son,

Jer

May 31, 2015: Time has permitted the courage to probe and the wisdom to recognize my shortcomings and truly appreciate Dad's remarkable attributes. It was a cultural and generational divide. Dad was a role model as a father and husband. He was the first of his family to leave the farm and work in a white-collar environment. He was a gentle, warm, and unassuming man with unparalleled character and integrity. His sense of love, devotion, and loyalty to his family and friends was unprecedented. Perhaps by sharing this letter, others may find peace and comfort in their personal relationships. Dad died at the age of ninety-three.

Jerome Domask

Jerome (Jerry) Domask is an active 75-year-old tri-athlete, Vietnam veteran, and retired Army officer with twenty years of service. His background is a kaleidoscope of professions and activities. He is an artist (painting, sculpting, and writing), former management consultant with Pricewaterhouse-Coopers, founder and CEO of the DoMar Group, and currently founder of Jerome Domask Fine Art.

Jerry expresses himself through art that requires the ability to present ideas visually and to document them for art exhibitions and accompanying publicity. His work is a constant search for originality and spontaneity in understanding his crafts, to use each new creation as steppingstone for subsequent growth. The evolution of his work tends to reflect raw energy, gestural images, and a daring to go places others hesitate to venture. It can run counter to an academic approach.

Jerry's return to the Far East during 2014 was accompanied by a request to document the trip with words and photos for a local newspaper. It was later published as an independent 40-page photo-journal story. Writing, to Jerry, is a difficult and demanding art form. It does not lend itself to the freedom he finds in painting or sculpture and presents a challenging experience that motivates him to expand his creative skills.

8

THE NEEDLE

Betsy Beard

She bent over her work in the dim light, struggling to see the pattern. She'd completed hundreds of projects just like this one, but her eyes were getting worse. The pattern wasn't complicated, just exacting, demanding her full attention. Her calloused fingers worked the needle for a few more minutes, pushing and pulling, pushing and pulling.

Finally she sat back with a sigh. The rest would have to wait; tomorrow was another day. As the candle sputtered, Betsy remembered the events that led to that first project years ago. It was important enough to keep her burning the midnight candles back then, capturing her imagination, and requiring artistry, precision, and concentration. It had been a few months after the death of her beloved John. And it was only because of John that the opportunity presented itself in the first place.

It's funny how fate interacts with our intentions, she thought. She really missed John, his kindness and goodness, his head for business, and his love for her. It was because of love that they had married, he the son of an Episcopal assistant rector at Christ Church and she the eighth of seventeen children born to good Quaker parents. She had first met John when her parents apprenticed her to an upholsterer. John was an apprentice that year, too. She surprised everyone by eloping with John, knowing full well that she would be read out of the Quaker church, lost to her family and friends. A pariah of sorts.

John and Betsy started their own upholstery shop with their meager savings a little while after the wedding. Between them they knew much about home fashion, designing bed linens, window curtains, slipcovers, chair cushions, and all manner of other needed items. But the business struggled: the colonies were in turmoil, fabric was scarce, and John had joined the militia to make a few extra shillings.

Betsy remembered how the city was filled with plots and counterplots, secret committees, and firebrand orators, enough to keep everyone uneasy, all 40,000 souls. Tom Payne had published his thoughts on tyranny and it seemed that everyone was swept up in independence fever.

It was a horror never to be forgotten that John was guarding the ammunition depot when it went up in flames that January. Betsy nursed his injuries as best she could, but he died shortly thereafter. Widowed by war, she determined to keep the shop open. There was little choice in the matter. Her birth family had rejected her.

That was the year the Continental Congress convened for the first time in Philadelphia. Betsy always felt it was because of John's connections that she was commissioned for that long-ago project. John's uncle was the Pennsylvania delegate to the Continental Congress, and the Ross family pew at Christ Church was right next to General Washington's pew. Betsy and John had even done piecework for the general, a few cravats and ruffles on his shirts. She never imagined that marrying John would take her in a direction to be acquainted with such important people.

It wasn't altogether surprising when John's uncle and General Washington showed up on her doorstep requesting her help making a flag that would fan the flames of freedom.

Washington, as the Commander in Chief of the colonial forces, needed newly designed standards and flags. The Continental Army deserved nothing less. When Washington had raised the colonies' Grand Union Flag on New Year's Day at Prospect Hill, the British actually thought the colonists were surrendering. With its British Union Jack in the upper left-hand corner, the Grand Union Flag was not distinctive enough to represent a free nation. It was time for a new banner.

Tonight as she laid her sewing aside, Betsy pondered the course of her life. In retrospect, it didn't even seem odd that she had been entrusted with that new design. After the War of Independence, many among the fairer sex were acknowledged for their skill and passion and cunning. Gender, she thought, does not make us incapable of rational thought, artful expression, or political passion.

In Edenton, Penelope Barker had instigated a boycott of British tea that was felt as keenly as the Tea Party in Boston. In Philadelphia itself, Esther Reed had formed the Philadelphia Association to sew shirts for the soldiers. Even Lydia Darragh, a Philadelphia Quaker and therefore opposed to getting involved in war, reported on a meeting in her house where she overheard the British planning a surprise attack, personally delivering the information to General Washington.

More than a few women had donned uniforms and were able to pass muster as soldiers—until an illness or injury was tended by a physician who clearly knew the difference. Others borrowed their husbands' clothing while the men were at war, stopping British couriers, spying on troops, and scouting shortcuts for the Continental Army. She'd even heard of one woman who insisted that the British officers join her for tea. While she entertained the officers, American troops were able to retreat unscathed.

Betsy sighed. She'd be here all night if she tried to remember all the things women had put their hearts and minds to doing so that the new nation could be born. She banked the fire and made her way to the stairs, carrying the sputtering candle.

It was decades ago that Betsy had made that first flag for the fledgling troops. She smiled as she remembered her audacity in suggesting they use a different star in place of the six-pointed star in Washington's design. He was surprised when she showed him how to fold the paper and make one snip to create a pattern for an evenly spaced five-pointed star. By now, she had made so many stars and flags she'd lost count.

So many years had gone by, each with its particular joys and sorrows, decisions and fates. Betsy had been widowed by war, not once but twice. And now she had outlived her third husband. As the stairs creaked under her slow tread, she pondered again the interweaving of intention and happenstance, choice and fate. She felt grateful to have been born in America, relieved that the turbulent times were past, and honored to be part of the flag-making community for almost fifty years.

Betsy never realized in the beginning that those stitches and those one-snip stars would become the subject of poets and songwriters. But now she was filled with pride that those broad stripes and bright stars had become a lasting symbol of courage for those who were willing to fight for freedom.

As she settled under the covers, Betsy Ross Ashburn Claypoole thought of the flag she would complete tomorrow, skillfully shaping a symbol for all to see.

"Truly," she said aloud, "We are born in a certain place at a specific time. And yes, fate plays a hand in our lives. But what we make of our time on earth is mostly in our own hands. As surely as my fingers have plied a needle for freedom, others have found different tools."

As for that new flag, the one she would deliver tomorrow, Betsy prayed a blessing on it as she closed her eyes, "Long may you wave o'er the land of the free and the home of the brave."

Betsy Beard

Betsy Beard's writing career began on October 14, 2004, immediately after notification that her only son, Specialist Bradley Scott Beard, had been killed in action in Ar Ramadi, Iraq. Finding some solace in pouring her heartache into a journal, she called it "hemorrhaging on paper."

Since that time, she has continued to write and has published articles in newspapers, *TAPS Magazine*, *Living with Loss Magazine*, and Hospice Foundation of America's 2008 *Living with Grief*, *2012 Journeys with Grief*, and *2013 Living with Grief*.

Betsy became the editor for *TAPS Magazine* in 2008. In 2010, she wrote the award-winning children's book, *Klinger, A Story of Honor and Hope*. The book earned gold medals from Moonbeam Children's Book Awards, Young Voices Foundation, and Military Writers Society of America (MWSA).

In addition to writing, Betsy has presented workshops on bereavement for the Department of Veterans Affairs' Regional and National Trainings and participated in the Casualty Notification training for the United States Army Casualty and Mortuary Affairs Operation Center (CMAOC).

Prior to the death of her son, Betsy worked in the banking industry, home-schooled her children through high school, and spent twenty-one years working in hospital laboratories as a medical technologist. She recently retired and lives in North Carolina with Randy, her husband of thirty-six years.

9

SYMBOL OF COURAGE

Jim Greenwald

tapestry

needle and thread
sweat and blood

row by row
stars and stripes began

baby steps to freedom
baby steps to exceptionalism

deep within us all hope burns

the weaving of our flag
the music of hope and courage for all

dance to each note

this journey holds hope close as courage blooms

[A nation of faults is not a nation at fault]

I remember

when
>I did not feel your steps upon me
>I did not feel the flames of your hatred

I remember
>waving proudly before all that could see
>everyone standing and honoring me

I remember
>times changing – pride turning to shame
>not being honored as I was in the past

when
>I became a symbol of a growing distaste
>I became an article of clothing

I know times change, people change
I did not realize liberty and justice would fall out of favor
but then – I am only a flag

I can only hope that pride will return
so little is needed, look inside for your courage
America is exceptional

Jim Greenwald

Having served in the Navy in a variety of capacities, whether he wanted to or not, Jim Greenwald enjoyed the opportunity to see much of the world and to meet two presidents. He holds degrees in computer science, business administration, and business management as well as a master's degree in human resource management and industrial relations. He has three children and four beautiful teenage granddaughters. He is a two-time survivor of cancer who enjoys each and every vertical day, crediting the Creator and a positive attitude for his survival. His writing is a reflection of his multicultural background: Ojibwe, French, and German.

Jim's poetry has been published extensively in e-zines, magazines, and anthologies nationally and internationally. He has published eleven books of poetry to date, mixing emotional poetry and Native American oriented poetry and stories. He has received several awards for his writing including five gold medals from Military Writers Society of America for his books titled *Tears for Mother Earth*, *Across the Bridge*, *Twisted Tongues* (which was also nominated for a Pushcart Prize), *Emotional Mélange*, and *Kings of the Green Jelly Moon: The Book*; a silver medal for the *Kings of the Green Jelly Moon: The CD;* and a bronze medal for *Sugar, Zeroes, and Lemon Drops*.

Jim's work has earned four Editor's Choice awards from the International Library of Poetry and two Honor Scroll Awards from Angels Without Wings Foundation. He is a lifetime member of Military Writers Society of America, Canadian Federation of Poets, American Authors Society, Academy of American Poets, and the Native American Rights Fund. He lives by a quiet stream in Bedford County, Pennsylvania, where he can hear the water speak.

10

ADJUSTING TO NEW REALITIES

Jim Tritten

In 1979, my life changed. I crashed a military airplane. It only took a few seconds, but the near-death experience would unequivocally and permanently alter the rest of my life. Relationships with my family, my work, and my view of myself would never be the same.

Post traumatic stress disorder was hardly even a figment in my imagination at the time, so I did not seek counseling nor was any seriously offered. Military medicine was embarrassingly negligent in 1979. A series of unexplained symptoms increased in severity until an extremely stressful incident in 2008 brought all my past unresolved issues to a head. I fell into a tailspin and retired unceremoniously from all work on a psychological disability. I was in total crisis, unable to function in society.

I became a professional patient and sought explanations for what was going on with my body and my mind. And in only a short time, I received a diagnosis. The good news: we knew the problem. The bad news: full blown post traumatic stress disorder was considered a mental illness.

Until you've experienced being diagnosed with mental illness, you have no idea how society treats such individuals. To merely read about the symptoms and the effects doesn't do it justice. So imagine yourself walking through a sunny parking lot. It's a Sunday afternoon, and you're out running errands. You see someone you know well—a leader in your community known for their political activism. You watch the individual make eye contact with you and then avert their eyes. The person ducks quickly into their car, turns the key, and drives off. Now picture this person wearing a clerical collar.

But I don't need to imagine. Such an event happened to me. The only thing I thought about later when I was processing what happened was maybe I should wear a sign, "don't worry, PTSD isn't contagious."

Successfully dealing with mental illness on your own is simply not possible. It's no easier than trying to walk on a broken foot without a crutch.

In 2008 following a total meltdown, I sought help from the VA. But being able to crack the nut of making a case, being correctly classified, approved, and then scheduled for treatment wasn't an easy task. Getting seen by the VA would take more than a year. In the meantime, I discovered the National Alliance on Mental Illness (NAMI) and took advantage of their support groups and classes.

I transitioned from initial diagnosis to being part of a new club. I learned what to do next with the aid of excellent clinicians, a well-developed program at the VA, and peers who volunteer with NAMI. I left my first prescription on the shelf for a month before I could muster the courage to take the first pill. I knew that once I did, my life would never be the same.

With help, I learned the path leading to a predictable and better end state. I mastered coping skills, gained knowledge, grew to tolerate medicines, and changed my environment. Group therapy allowed me to see fragile souls blossom as they met with like individuals who suffered the same judgment by society, friends, and family. These folks deal with unjustified inner shame and share hope for a better life.

I discovered there are "underground" support groups where veterans go when they don't want PTSD on their work record. I empathized with them and told my story of being first diagnosed in 1993 and hiding the branding so I could continue to work. That is...until meltdown. I show them the results of not seeking treatment. The choice is theirs. At the time it happened to me, I didn't understand the choice.

I write for therapy. I don't want to write about my trauma and I don't want to write about the negative aspects of my diagnosis and treatment. Instead, I focus on humor and enjoy it when I write a piece that can make others (and me) laugh. I learned a lot from the VA about emotions. First, to recognize there are emotions other than anger. Second, to be able to describe what goes on inside myself when I feel other emotions. The last bit is tricky—how to write words that will cause the reader to feel the emotion that I felt and am now trying to describe. From writing things that will make you laugh, my goal is to write about things that will make you cry.

I share my story with veterans and non-veterans alike. I know it's customary for vets to say no one but another vet can understand the challenges of military service. I differ with that opinion. I've obtained excellent care from mental health professionals who've never been in the military or crashed an airplane. I also learn from individuals diagnosed with a variety of mental illnesses that have nothing to do with PTSD. But they all face the same issues I faced, like being shunned by people they know. We debate if it is easier to keep your old friends or make new ones.

I volunteer my time to lead support groups for individuals with all types of mental illnesses. I learn from them, and we help each other. One of my volunteer activities includes going into the high-security mental health units at a county jail. Incarcerated patients in my support groups include my fellow vets, both men and women. Not everyone has what it takes to do volunteer work inside a jail, but it's a great opportunity for vets who do have what it takes.

We discuss issues common to anyone with any mental illness. How to get the support of family and what to do when support does not come. How do we define recovery? Who else has stopped taking their medicine and not told anyone? Will this PTSD ever go away? How best to process the trauma?

We live in a country where there finally are good tools to deal with PTSD and good programs to reach all veterans who are branded with this diagnosis. The VA and NAMI are both organizations that offer hope to people like me who needed to be shown the road to recovery. With help, recovery is possible—and I define recovery as being able to function as well as I can, given the cards I've been dealt. No, my world is not the same as it was when I could work, let alone when I was a navy pilot. My new environment is smaller and less complex. And it involves working on my diagnosis every day for the rest of my life. My new reality.

As veterans with a diagnosis, we have the opportunity to get good treatment and share what we learn at the VA with those less fortunate than we. We can help ourselves as we help others. Hope multiplies as each of us comes to terms with our new reality and reaches out to help another.

Jim Tritten

Jim retired after a 44-year career with the department of defense including duty as a carrier-based naval aviator. He holds advanced degrees from the university of Southern California and formerly served as a faculty member and National Security Affairs Department Chair at the Naval Postgraduate School.

Jim's publications have won him thirteen writing awards, including the Alfred Thayer Mahan award from the Navy League of the United States and the annual Department of Veterans Affairs National Veterans Creative Arts Festivals. He has published five books, twenty chapters, and 251 articles and government technical reports. Jim has been a frequent speaker at many military and international conferences and has seen his work translated into Russian, French, Spanish, and Portuguese.

A recipient of the Eagle Scout award as a teenager, Jim has been active throughout his entire life as a volunteer, board member, and officer in numerous national, state, and local organizations. He was recently awarded the National Alliance on Mental Illness (NAMI) connection leadership award for his volunteer efforts throughout New Mexico on behalf of individuals diagnosed with mental illnesses.

Jim has completed a mystery, *Fatal Waters,* set in Sandoval County, New Mexico, along the Rio Puerco. Jim's main character is a Hispanic male Navy pilot veteran who, like Jim, is combating post traumatic stress disorder while dealing with numerous unforeseen problems.

11

IT'S NOT ABOUT WHAT YOU'VE LOST

Joyce Faulkner

It was a large area filled with treadmills and exercise equipment. Like all gyms, a dozen or more beautiful people lifted weights, did abdominal crunches, and stretched their sore muscles. Most wore sweatshirts, shorts, and tennis shoes. Some worked with a trainer.

Others went through carefully choreographed routines designed to maximize their physical prowess. Each focused inward—intent on achieving some personal goal. The only difference between this room and thousands of others scattered across the country was that these young men and women were wounded soldiers and marines, newly returned from Iraq and Afghanistan.

I stood in the doorway gripping a canvas bag filled with books and journals.

"Excuse me." The voice behind me was respectful.

I turned. A tall boy sitting in a wheelchair waited for me to move out of his way. One leg was missing just below the knee. The other was propped out in front of him, splinted and skewered and pinned together. His foot was bare, the toes black and yellow.

"Oh, I'm sorry." I moved out of the way, sorry for many things. He smiled as the nurse pushed him past me and into the room.

My friend, Eddie Beesley, a Vietnam veteran who is a double amputee, rolled up to the young marine and shook his hand. Connie, Eddie's wife, chattered like a canary. Her bubbly presence filled the room with light. The two of them worked together—encouraging and inspiring. I admired them. They were already touching hearts.

I was frozen, my eyes still locked on the horrendous wounds. A pretty black woman sat on a large sheet-covered cushion. Her skin glowed in the florescent lighting. Her left thigh ended in an elasticized sleeve. Her right leg was smooth and well-toned, just like her left one had been a few months ago. A boy in an electric wheelchair zoomed past. He was missing both legs, an arm, and three fingers of his remaining hand.

I shook off my shyness and began to hand out journals, encouraging each person to use it to write down his thoughts for his children. Some reached for them eagerly. One young soldier said he wished he'd had one sooner. Another thanked me and tucked it into a large pocket in his backpack. I watched him walk away on his new legs. A few feet away, he paused to flirt with a cute girl who'd just come into the room.

A beefy marine wanted the journal to keep track of his reps. He was a weightlifter before he'd been hurt. It was different now, but he was still a weightlifter. He flexed a massive bicep to show me.

An amputee in his thirties sat beside his wife, massaging his stump. She held his brand new prosthesis. I handed him a journal. Connie introduced herself and launched into all the ways she and Eddie had dealt with disability.

"No matter what they say, you can still have a waterbed if you want one," she said. "Just be aware of the challenges and decide if you want to deal with them."

The man nodded and his wife put her hand on his shoulder. With just a few words, Connie made everyone realize that as awful as these wounds are, these young people are still vital, still sexy, still powerful, still alive.

As we left, the soldier in the electric wheelchair zipped past us again. This time, I didn't see his afflictions, but the mischievous sparkle of an eighteen-year-old boy. We waved at him as the elevator doors closed.

Joyce Faulkner

Joyce Faulkner has been writing and winning awards since she was fifteen, publishing her first article while she was still in high school. Her writing credentials include many magazine, newspaper, and web articles, both literary and technical. She is a web, newspaper, and book designer, as well as an author, ghostwriter, publisher, and editor.

Joyce's educational background includes a major in writing at the University of Arkansas, a bachelor's degree in Chemical Engineering from the University of Pittsburgh, and an MBA from Cleveland State University.

Published books include *Windshift, Username, Chance ... and Other Horrors, Role Call: Women's Voices* (with Pat McGrath Avery), *Sunchon Tunnel Massacre Survivors* (with Pat McGrath Avery), *In the Shadow of Suribachi, For Shrieking Out Loud, Losing Patience*, and *Paragraphs: Mysteries of the Golden Booby* (with Bob Doerr, David Harry, and Pat McGrath Avery).

12

MARCH OF COURAGE

Beth Underwood

Dave Thomas couldn't remember if he'd always been a homebody or if he'd chosen to be one. Which wasn't to say he never left home. Far from it. Uncle Sam sent him across the pond to Iraq where he'd served his country with pride. But these days, he didn't like to leave home. If it weren't for his mandatory visits to the VA hospital, he'd have been content to stay there.

So he was already out of his comfort zone by the time he pulled out of his driveway, and his nerves were shot before he made it out of the county. He was headed ninety miles east, from Sweetwater to Gatlinburg, Tennessee. Once there, Dave would meet up with Gold Star parents Tim and Marsha Hunt. After a night's sleep, he would walk in honor and remembrance of their son Joey and another fellow soldier at the annual Mountain Man Memorial March.

While he wasn't sure what ultimately caused him to make the trek east on that particular April weekend, Dave knew it was the right thing to do, even if almost ten years had passed since his life changed. He didn't remember much about that day long past—two anti-tank mines detonated under the new humvee he was riding in—only that in the aftermath the heat from the asphalt felt as if it was burning his flesh. But he wanted to remember the details. So he carried a copy of the book that chronicled the story of his platoon and the story of that day. And whenever anyone asked what happened, he let them read it for themselves.

What he knew for sure was that two good men died that day. Some days he laments that it was his fault, that there was something he could've done to stop the IED. Most days, he doesn't understand why he survived and struggles to find a purpose, some sort of meaning to his life. Comfort comes from a bottle of Jack Daniels and a newfound relationship with God. Some people say he can't drink and know who God is. Dave says different, that God understands how a war-hardened soldier sometimes needs a few nips from that bottle to calm the pain and keep the demons away.

Dave was often perplexed by the notion that Tim and Marsha Hunt didn't hate him—their son Joey was one of the men who died that day Dave didn't. But the truth was that the Hunts yearned to be with the ones who'd lived. Because seeing them and talking to them helped them feel closer to Joey. In the grand scheme of things, the soldiers who survived that day helped the Hunts chase away their own demons.

As the sun broke over the top of the mountain on the morning of the march, a thousand men and women—many of them soldiers carrying full rucksacks—took off on the 26.2 mile hike. Tim took photos while Marsha and Dave waited for the bulk of the crowd to thin out before joining in.

They walked for about fifteen minutes, making it past dozens of the downtown businesses that would soon be filled with tourists. For now, though, the streets and stores were empty. Dave needed a break, and removing the prosthetic limb that accounted for three quarters of his left leg would provide a few minutes' relief. While he rested, he told Tim and Marsha how honored he was to be there. He thought of how he'd have given his other leg, too, if it meant Joey could've lived. He pulled out his bottle of isopropyl alcohol and sprayed the suction liner of the prosthesis. He reattached the socket, and headed back to starting line with Marsha Hunt, all the while apologizing that he hadn't been able to walk further.

But right now Dave needed to get home. If he didn't get there soon, he'd run out of the temporary relief granted by his pain medications. Once that happened, it would be almost impossible to get on the other side of the pain.

There was always next year, he told himself. Next year, maybe the pain wouldn't be as bad.

Beth Underwood

A native Kentuckian from the small town of Cynthiana, Beth Underwood holds an abiding love for the United States of America and those who defend her. The daughter of a Vietnam flight surgeon and niece of a World War II radioman, she has always been fascinated with American military history, from the stories of the American Revolution and writings of the Founding Fathers to the modern wars of the 21st Century.

During high school, Beth traveled abroad with the Foreign Study League and American Institute of Foreign Study. Her time in Europe took her to the hallowed grounds of Dachau concentration camp, fueling her passion for World War II history.

Oddly enough, her first college degree came in the unlikely field of architecture, where she spent thirteen years. Luckily, she returned to her senses and embraced her love of storytelling, receiving her degree in journalism and re-launching her career as a writer.

After the tragic events of 9/11, her writing began to focus solely on stories of the men and women of United States Armed Forces. Her work has appeared in numerous newspapers and magazines over the past twenty years. Among her accolades, she was the recipient of MWSA's 2010 People's Choice Award. In March of 2015, her first book, *Gravity*, was published by Red Engine Press. As she looks to the future, she plans to continue preserving the stories of America's heroes. She currently lives in central Kentucky with her son Colton and their German Shepherd, Stryker.

Army National Guard veteran David Thomas at the 2015 Mountain Man Memorial March, walking in honor of Victoir Lieurance and Joey Hunt who were killed in action on August 22, 2005. Photo by Beth Underwood

13

OVERCOMING FEAR

By Ray Schumack

It was June 1950. I was twenty-two years old, untested in many ways, working nights as a copyboy at the *New York Times*. I was teaching myself during my dinner hour how to use one of the old Underwood typewriters that sat on every reporter's desk when news arrived telling us North Korean troops had invaded South Korea.

Very shortly I found myself drafted, wearing green fatigues, and training at Fort Devens in Massachusetts, learning how to use an M-1 rifle, 30- and 50-caliber machine guns, bazookas, and hand grenades. It was fun, especially near the end of training when we learned how to climb telephone poles wearing pole climbers. When training ended, we were on our way to Korea as combat wiremen. Suddenly it wasn't fun anymore.

Arriving one night in the dark at a compound near Seoul, we fell exhausted onto cots in a tent and were soon asleep. We awoke the next morning in what looked like a concentration camp surrounded by barbed wire. A young lieutenant arrived and told us we were in the 3rd Infantry Division's Repo Depot. He approached me carrying papers on a clipboard.

"I see you worked as an editorial assistant at the *New York Times*," he said.

"Yes, Sir," I replied, hiding the fact I had slightly enhanced my resume.

"And you can type," the lieutenant added.

"That's right," I answered without hesitation, almost certain I was not going to wind up a combat wireman. I did learn later there were no telephone poles left to climb in Korea at that time.

"How would you like to be a combat correspondent writing for *Stars and Stripes*?" he asked.

"Great," I said trying to hide my surprise and pleasure. What luck! I couldn't hope for a better assignment.

Next morning I left for 3rd Division HQ Forward in a jeep carrying mail. It was a one-hour ride to the combat area. Along the route there were woods and abandoned villages. Suddenly I was frightened.

"What am I doing?" I asked myself. "Here I am wearing a steel helmet and carrying a 30-caliber automatic carbine. Could a sniper get me? Will I come under artillery fire?" For the first time the thought of not making it home entered my mind.

We arrived at the forward headquarters area and found it in disarray, like a scene in an old World War II movie. Troops were striking tents, rolling them up, and loading them—along with boxes, files, and typewriters—onto trucks. I asked for the officer in charge of PIO (Public Information Office) and was introduced to Captain Robert Downey, a soft-spoken, gentle 35-year-old World War II veteran.

Half the men in Korea were like that—older veterans with families, called back to active duty—and the other half were like me, young boys who had just missed serving in World War II.

The PIO contingent packed its gear and took off for its new location. Once there we found we would be sitting in front of a battery of noisy 155-mm howitzers.

As we set up our tents and equipment, a first sergeant approached me. A 20-year career man with graying hair, a tall stocky build, and a gravelly voice, he reminded me of actor Ward Bond who played sergeants in director John Ford's western movies with John Wayne. "You're the new boy here today so you have guard duty tonight, midnight to 0800," he said as he walked away to see that everything was being unloaded and unpacked properly.

There was no moonlight that night. Our tents were set up in a cul-de-sac in front of a paddy field now slightly frozen by the cool night air. I walked around the cul-de-sac holding a carbine against my chest.

Suddenly I heard rustling sounds coming from the paddy field behind our tents. I stood still and the noise stopped. I thought of stories I heard about Chinese soldiers creeping up on American soldiers in their sleeping bags and stabbing them with bayonets. Chills ran down my spine. When I took another step the noise continued. When I stood still the noise stopped again. Soon I could hear only my heart beating.

What if I fired a warning shot to awaken everyone and there was nothing in the paddy field? What a jerk I'd be. No one would talk to me after that. What if I did nothing and some of us were killed? All my training gave me no answers. Would I have the courage to do the right thing?

About 6:00 a.m. the sky began to lighten. In the paddy field, I could now see about a dozen mice scampering around creating rustling sounds.

How silly it was that a family of mice, rather than our enemy, had scared me out my wits, leaving my heart pounding. My fears conquered, I now found the courage to visit frontline troops every other day, spending the alternate days at my Underwood typewriter producing that day's news story or feature article, mostly concentrating on the oddball things men do in combat to overcome their fears. I preferred to make my soldier readers laugh rather than focus on blood and guts events.

I learned two things in Korea. First, war is a terrible waste of young men's minds, bodies, and lives. Second, visiting United Nations' troops from many different counties, I saw that there was very little difference in our fears, hopes, courage, and love for families.

Author's note: Stories about war and great battles have described heroism in combat while others described destruction, suffering, death, and dismemberment of young men's bodies. Less has been written about the human condition—the need for companionship and trust, the strange and sometimes funny things men do in combat. This is the humanity the author struggled to find and write about as an Army combat correspondent in Korea.

Ray Schumack

Ray Schumack was born in the Bronx and attended New York City public grammar schools. Later he moved to Queens where his family remained until after he graduated from Fordham University. Ray had no idea what kind of work he wanted to do until, by chance, he applied for a job at the *New York Times*. He studied how reporters wrote, learned how a daily newspaper was produced, and fell in love with journalism.

Following military service, Ray held positions as a magazine editor, a publicity director, and an account manager for a Madison Avenue public relations agency. He served for fifteen years as chief communications officer in the headquarters of a Fortune 500 company, responsible for the company's corporate communications and the product promotion for seventeen divisions worldwide. His business articles have appeared in the *Wall Street Journal*, the *New York Times*, *Fortune Magazine* and many professional publications. He also served as an adjunct professor at Long Island University and later lectured at Columbia Graduate School of Journalism. On retiring from the business world he established his own public relations firm and continues to serve several clients.

Ray's experience as a combat correspondent writing for *Stars and Stripes* during the Korean War became the subject of his book, *News Dispatches from the Korean War*, dedicated to his three children: Barrie, Sharon Ann, and Daniel. All of them heard more than once a few of the stories recounted in the book.

14

OPERATION HUSKY

Susan May

North Africa 1943

Troop Carrier Command

Captain Russell Giles gripped the yoke of the C-47 transport plane. As pilot he carried the responsibility for the eighteen paratroopers who were his cargo on this mission. His crew of four had mentally and physically prepared for this flight for months in the desert of North Africa.

The living conditions he and the rest of the 314th Troop Carrier Wing of the Ninth Air Force had lived under hadn't worked in their favor. Along with sand and bugs of every type and temperatures in Tunisia reaching over a hundred and the Sirocco wind blowing continually, the men found it a hardship just trying to eat and sleep. Russell didn't even want to think about the last time he'd had a good meal.

"Hey, Wilky, do you know where we are?" Russell radioed the navigator as he looked out the side window for some sign of the other planes participating in the invasion of Hitler's underbelly.

Russell groaned. It was 0500 and pitch black outside. The Mediterranean Sea lay below them full of Navy ships, and Sicily lay ahead where the Italian and German armies waited. They were already facing tough times and didn't need to add being lost.

"I see the lights of Malta off to our left, Captain." Mitchell, his navigator, came back.

That was good. The people of Malta had been asked to burn their light on this date so the planes could use the island halfway between Africa and Sicily as a landmark. Still, night flying gave new meaning to the idea of flying blind. It took courage.

Russell nodded toward the back of the plane and asked his co-pilot Erwin, "How're our passengers doing?"

"Comfortable. Some, I think, are asleep."

"Good. If it's even a little bit like the brass expects, they may not rest again for months."

It seemed like days ago though it had only been hours since they had sat in the briefing tent listening to the brass explain the mission plan. The flight surgeon circled the room and made sure every man ate cookies and drank juice. Russell hadn't been hungry but took them anyway, not knowing when he might get to eat again.

They had a few more hours of flight time before they would reach their destination. All he had to do was hold the plane steady and stay in formation. Doing so left too much time to think of home. He hadn't seen his mother and father in a year and a half. His mother wrote him regularly. Just to get a letter lifted his spirits. Yesterday, he'd received one from Jane. They had been friends since childhood and had even started talking about getting married when the Japanese bombed Pearl Harbor. He couldn't bring himself to make any promises before he left. Still she wrote him faithfully and that gave him something to hope for when the war was over.

Mitchell's calm voice came over the speaker. "Captain, we're thirty minutes out from the coast."

"Okay, let's take her down to a hundred feet." Russell pushed the yoke forward in a slow steady motion. Erwin followed his lead. "That's it. Level off."

The hum of the engines and the vibration on the plane blended with the rapid beat of Russell's heart as they closed in on their target. He knew his job, had done it more than a few times, but most of his crew were green and had never been tested under fire.

"Look." Erwin pointed out the windshield at the bright flash from a Navy gun below. The sky lit up as other shells went off.

The plane bounced, buffeted by an explosion. The rising sun and gunfire smoke made visibility low. They were approaching the beach when another loud explosion ripped the air.

"Hold it steady, Erwin. We have to get through this before we can make the drop zone three miles inland."

A shell exploded to the right. Russell clutched the yoke making an effort to hold the plane level. "That one was too close."

"Yeah. Wallace wasn't so lucky," Erwin yelled.

The plane next to them had lost part of a wing and was going down. Would any of the men survive? He knew the crew in the downed plane. He'd shared a table in the mess tent with them just hours ago. Another shot burst beside them. In horror Russell watched another plane hit the water.

"Oh my God! Our own guys are shooting at us!" Erwin's voice was high and thin with disbelief.

Some of the paratroopers started yelling. Fear lodged in Russell's throat. With no radio contact between planes or the ground, they were at the mercy of God to see that they survived.

"Erwin, pay attention to your job," Russell said in a firm calm voice that didn't match the turmoil within him. He had no choice but to continue in the same pattern. Flying so low and at such a slow speed made his plane a huge lumbering target but there was a mission to complete.

Shells burst around them. Sometimes they were so close that Russell was blinded by the light for a second.

"We need to get the hell out of here, Captain," Mitchell called.

"Settle down and concentrate on your job, Mitchell. Fifteen minutes to green light, Chief."

"Roger, Captain," Marks, his crew chief, came back.

As they passed the beach, the German and Italian guns zeroed in on them, but thankfully none found their mark. The drop zone lay just ahead.

"Give them the green light," Russell said, his attention never leaving the sky in front of him.

Erwin flipped on the switch on the overhead console. Russell had no doubt that the light was glowing brightly in the fuselage. Chief would tell the sergeant of the paratroopers they were over the jump zone. The men would stand up and hook up to the line running the length of the plane. Seconds later men would begin jumping out of the side door of the plane with their parachutes opening above them.

It was light outside now. Shells and shots continue to fill the sky coming from gun emplacements in olive groves or built into the sun-bleached landscape. With all the paratroopers out, Russell pulled back on the yoke and gained attitude as he circled back toward the coast. As he moved out over the water, fighting raged below. He couldn't think about those men. His job at that time was to see that he, his crew, and their plane returned to the airfield in Tunisia. There the aircraft would be reloaded with supplies, and hours later Russell and his crew would make the journey back to Sicily.

This would happen over and over again until the small island off the Italian coast was under Allied control and the course of World War II would turn.

Author's note: Because of the friendly fire issue during the offensive into Italy, black and white stripes were required on all planes during the Normandy invasion, so the same mistake would never be made again.

Susan May

Susan May is a graduate of Auburn University with a degree in Political Science. She lives in Georgia. Susan and her husband have four grown children and twin grandchildren. When she is not writing she loves to travel, sew, enjoy afternoon teas, visit castles, and read voraciously.

She is a multi-published author. Her first book *Nick's New Heart* about her son's heart transplant at the age of two was released in 2008. He is now twenty-six. She has also written numerous books of fiction published through HarperCollins.

As an avid history buff, Susan is fascinated by the sites and history of World War II. Through the National World War II Museum's travel program, Susan followed the United States victors' path from England to Normandy into Germany. On a separate trip, she visited Malta, Sicily, and mainland Italy following the Allies' invasion path in 1943. Another journey took her to the South Pacific to visit battle sites on Hawaii, Guam, Saipan, including a day trip to the island of Iwo Jima.

Writing as S. Carlisle May, she has authored *A World War II Flight Surgeon's Story* published by Pelican Publishing. This book shines a light on one of the many unsung heroes of World War II. The book is based on her personal interviews with the subject of the book, Dr. Lamb Myhr, his personal letters home during the war, and photographs he took while in North Africa, Normandy, and Germany. It was published in May 2015.

15

THE STATION DOES NOT FORGET

Joe Carvalko

The station does not forget

bright-eyed rolled recruits,
who return on rails,
less a few stragglers,
belated,
let's not stray,
over who lost their way.
It hears the dissonance
of laughter,
horns of sorrow,
swoosh,
the locomotive's legato breath,
whooshing out of time,

tubas over intonations,

roared arrivals,
those who return,
to mend,

lives,
born again,
or buried
under a cypress tree.
The "delivered,"
and those that missed homecoming,
to vacant platforms,
to echoed dins of patriotic fervor,
the station does not forget;

haunt-full reverberations,

pubescent voices,
rung revelry,
goodbyes waved,
while rucked old men,
in three piece suits,
moved letters
on parchment,
for parochial pursuits,
to mediate
a so-called peace,
and regretted that war subsided at all.
The station does not forget,

jingled coins, consternation

lost in the heave of a locomotive's gut,
lumbering into the station,
over oom pah pahs,
of a high school band.
Can't see the vet,
hand to brow,

or the twosome that trembles
near the charnel car,
inserted between Pullmans.
In time the train chuffs,
its legato strains trailing off,
emptied,

bright-eyed bandsmen box horns,

stationmaster bellows,
"Eastbound Track 9, N'York 'n points south,"
the blind, who now see, repeat,
"Hey, buddy, got two bits?"
'til drowned by a local that rumbles
into the funerary,
where broods who blow taps,
will soon beg handouts, or worse,
now honor,
flag-draped caskets,
fated for the necropolis
of crescents, crosses, and six-pointed stars.

The station does not forget.

Joe Carvalko

Joe Carvalko is an American author and lawyer born in Bridgeport, Connecticut. His recent novel, *We Were Beautiful Once: Chapters from a Cold War* was inspired by a trial he conducted that was featured in a 2004 documentary *Missing, Presumed Dead: The Search for America's POWs* narrated by Ed Asner. The book was a finalist in the MWSA category of historical fiction. He also recently authored *The Techno-human Shell: A Jump in the Evolutionary Gap*, about how future medical technology will transform us into part cyborg.

In 2004 Joe authored *A Deadly Fog*, a collection of poems, essays, and short stories about war in America. In 2007 he authored *A Road Once Traveled: Life from All Sides*, a narrative on the fabric of American life. In addition, Joe has authored numerous articles and academic papers. In 2012, he was one of two finalists for the Red Mountain Press, top poetry honors for "The Interior" and one of three finalists for the 2012 Esurance Poetry prize for "The Road Home." Recently he co-authored *Law, The Science and Technology Guidebook for Lawyers*.

When not writing, Joe is an adjunct professor of law at Quinnipiac University, School of Law, a member of the Community Bioethics Forum, Yale School of Medicine, and a member of the Yale Technology and Ethics working group, and the ABA Section on Science and Technology. Joe is also a jazz pianist (releasing a CD of standards in 2013) and a U.S. Air Force veteran. He, his wife Susie, and three cats divide their time between the Connecticut and Florida coastal areas.

Photo by U.S. Army Signal Corps, courtesy of Golden Gate NRA Park Archives

16

THE COURAGE TO HOPE

Sandra Miller Linhart

I want to tell you something, but I don't know where to begin. Do I start when my life as I knew it ended? Or, do I begin when an ember of hope rekindled the ashen remains of my wife's heart?

I've been watching over her since the moment I left; at her side every minute of every day. I stood beside her when they gave her the news. I yearned to hold her, to comfort her during the funeral as sobs racked her body and she fell apart on the casket.

Over the years, I've watched her stumble through life's tasks and responsibilities as she struggled to cope with my physical absence. I've answered her call of my name in the lonely, coldness of night, countless nights. And, although she couldn't feel it, I've pressed her trembling lips to mine. Every. Single. Day. She cried the tears I couldn't. I've smelled the soft fragrance of each tear as it coursed a path down her cheek, helpless to wipe any away or make them cease.

My soul aches for her healing. Her numbness becomes my reality as I am bound to her by the pure, delicate misery of love lost but not forgotten.

We are both prisoners here inside her grief.

But, a strange thing just happened. Someone bumped into her on the sidewalk and spilled her coffee. I sensed she was annoyed. Mad, almost. The man insisted on buying her another cup.

I felt her panic, wanting to say no.

I held her hand, and whispered, "Yes."

"Yes," she said, and sat down at a table.

Did I just hear her heart skip a beat?

Yes, I believe I did.

Her eyes smile at the stranger sitting across the table.

She laughs?

Yes, she laughs.

The melody of it tickles my being and releases this grip of sadness over our souls.

I sense a spark of hope, growing stronger inside her with each passing moment: with every smile, every laugh. I feel joy, and I feel the love: never-ending, all encompassing... and so healing. It's been a while since we felt that way.

I started this story at the end of mine. Now, the rest of this tale is hers for the telling.

I hope it's a love story.

***

SECOND CHANCE

She answered the phone.
A voice...
Strange, yet familiar, greeted her.
They spoke quite a while.
A hope...
Small, yet persistent; blossoming...
A soul encounter;
A chance,
Or something more divinely timed?
A requested date.
Courage.
...Where in the hell did she put that?

Sandra Miller Linhart

Born and raised in Lander, Wyoming, Sandra Linhart was a part of the United States Army community for over twenty years. She has five daughters, and seven grandkids, and currently resides in the beautiful mountains of Colorado.

Sandra's formal education includes CA Barstow College, where she studied and excelled in Art & Design, as well as receiving a degree in Sociology, focusing on family and child psychology, both of which were of great use to her when she had children of her own. Ms. Linhart also attended the University of Georgia, where she received certificates in Private Investigation and Creative Writing.

She is the author of the award-winning picture books *Daddy's Boots*, *Momma's Boots*, and *Pickysaurus Mac*, and the award-winning chapter-book series, *The Elementary Adventures of Jones, JEEP, Buck & Blue*. Other published titles include her picture books *But...What If?* and *Grandpa, What If?* addressing separation and reunion anxiety caused by deployment. *Mixed Up* assists children in learning and exploring their diverse ancestry. *Don't Label Me* is a book about bullying, and *Stackable Paige* explores early signs of OCD in toddlers.

Sandra is a member of the Society of Children's Book Writers and Illustrators and Military Writers Society of America. Look for her upcoming titles: *What Does a Hero Look Like?*; *When I Grow Up*; *Oh My! What Happened?*; *Squat*; *Sophe's on the Sofa*; *Hallie of the Harvey Houses*; *Stuck in the Middle with Jones, JEEP, Buck & Blue*; *Diary of an Unkempt Woman*; *Peace of Heaven*; and *Living with LV Brown*.

17

WHISPERS OF HOPE AND COURAGE

Kim Kluxen Meredith

"This is the man you are going to marry." My first whisper in 1977 transformed me into a best friend, a wife, and a mother. I thought maybe the sound in my head was coming from the speakers in my old Ford LTD as I drove home from the commuter train station, so I turned off my car radio. I didn't want the whole world to hear this private message. But I later learned that it was a whisper, and that it was intended only for my ears.

In the months to follow, I was courted with fresh lobsters packed in seaweed, brought to me by a handsome third-year law student and U.S. Navy Reservist. The live crustaceans, nestled in cardboard boxes, were stowed in the back of his squadron's P-3A Orion after a routine weekend flight to the Naval Air Station Brunswick, Maine. That base was home to a number of Navy-operated maritime patrol aircraft at the time. (I have since learned that the last plane left in 2009 and the runways permanently closed in 2010.)

Still in his olive-green flight suit and aviator sunglasses, this man also once carried into my apartment several wooden crates filled with clanking bottles of delicious red wine. He purchased them in a small shop near the Naval Station Rota,

Spain, another popular destination for his crew. "The Gateway to the Mediterranean," as that base was known, provided the perfect romantic libations for the two of us.

The clever tactics of this resourceful man worked, and the whisper came true. David Stewart Kluxen Jr. and I were married on September 3, 1977. The future was bright with hope.

***

"Get married again" were the words that my husband mouthed from his oscillating hospital bed in the neuro-intensive care unit.

I did not want to listen to this whisper. I was too full of fear to process my soulmate's desire. David was involved in a one-car accident that left him a quadriplegic. For the past thirteen days, I commuted to Thomas Jefferson University Hospital in Philadelphia to be by his side, and I was exhausted. This hospital was the East Coast Regional Spinal Cord Center and represented his only hope for survival.

We both knew that our time together was coming to an end, and we tried hard to accept our fate. He recognized that I had many more years of love to share. I was only forty years old, so my husband of fifteen years courageously offered me his permission for future happiness with another man. But I did not want to accept his generous gift. I only wanted him.

When David died on February 24, 1993, I wept. I didn't know how I was going to parent our two young children alone and console his son who was finishing his fourth year of college. I was scared. I wanted to turn back the clock and start all over with a lobster dinner and a glass of wine.

In the following years I thought about David's courage. He must have been so frightened when he woke up in his hospital bed after the accident, unable to move anything other than the muscles of his face. His incredibly sharp mind must have been racing faster than the planes he navigated. He expressed remorse and guilt for an event that was out of his control. His courage to ask me to help him die in his final days was beyond my comprehension. He provided advanced directives for his clients, but he never got around to preparing his own. He was only forty-four years old. He was so brave. All I could offer was my unconditional love. I did not feel any hope. I did not feel any courage.

Hope and courage need each other. Hope shines the light into the future and courage supplies the fuel to keep it burning brightly. During our marriage, when one faltered, the other stepped up. One gave and the other received. Courage offered strength; hope turned that force into opportunity.

Since David's death I have learned to listen to and trust my inner voice, my whispers. These messages from my heart have given me courage to do things that I never thought I could do. They have given me hope for a joy filled future.

In 2004, I finally accepted David's offer and remarried. He was right. I had more love to share.

We both needed hope and courage.

I still do.

Kim Kluxen Meredith

Kim Kluxen Meredith credits her colorful childhood in the small town of Ames, New York, for her strong character which she later had to call upon when she was widowed at the age of forty. Her book, *Listen for the Whispers: Coping with Grief and Learning to Live Again*, won a 2013 MWSA silver medal in the spiritual/religious category. It chronicles her healing journey after the untimely death of her husband David, a retired Navy flyer.

Kim received a bachelor's degree in Spanish from Washington College, which included a year of study at the University of Madrid. She furthered her education as a commercial litigation paralegal in Philadelphia, where she met her late husband. Kim retired from teaching high school Spanish in 2014, after twenty-five years in the classroom.

Her book is a resource for many grief support groups including the Open to Hope Foundation, for whom she writes articles and has two archived radio broadcasts. She presents workshops for Soaring Spirits International and posts monthly inspirational blog stories on her website. Kim has two published stories in the *Chicken Soup for the Soul* series and is working on her next book, a memoir of her small-town life.

A full-time freelance writer, Kim lives in Lancaster, Pennsylvania, with her husband Tom and enjoys trips to the New Jersey shore and time with her "best buddies," her three grandchildren.

David S. Kluxen, photo courtesy of Kim Kluxen Meredith

18

LIFE OR DEATH DECISION

Bill McDonald

In the spring of 1967, in an area about thirty-five miles northwest of Saigon, I had to make one of the biggest decisions of my life. We had been flying solo flights, mostly supply runs into small encampments of the 1st Infantry Division. The troops were there to slow down the movement of supplies that were coming directly from North Vietnam off the Ho Chi Minh Trail. There had been some fighting, but not nearly as bloody as we had expected.

Our intelligence reports indicated that we should be on the lookout for large movements of both supplies and troops, so we had been keeping a watchful eye on anything that moved on the ground. We hadn't received any hostile fire during the morning operations.

My helicopter commander was a major who had just arrived from a tour of several years in Germany. He was a West Point graduate and was strictly by the book, a real "no nonsense" type of guy with little sense of humor. When he gave an order, he expected full obedience. He didn't want to foster any friendships between himself and lower ranking souls in the unit. He was in charge, he was "the man," and we were there to support and obey his orders. That was the way things were.

During his first weeks in Nam, the major was still trying to figure out how to find the LZs and how to read the maps.

He didn't know the names of places we had to fly to, and he didn't know where these places were in relation to our base camp. Without a map in his hand, this guy wouldn't have any clue where we were. Yet he asked very few questions, if any.

On this particular morning, we were flying higher than felt comfortable to me—not at our normal treetop-level altitude. The major had an aversion to flying too close to the ground. He did not yet realize the risks that flying at higher altitudes presented. Eventually he would learn that flying at treetop level was actually much safer. We could sneak up on enemy troops well before they could see or hear us coming, the common procedure in Nam—fly low and fast. Keep your profile close to the ground.

From our lofty position in the sky, we could see much farther around the countryside. I think it may have been helpful for him in spotting landmarks. We did have a greater view of all that was down below, but it also made us an easier target. We weren't high enough to avoid small-arms fire and weren't low enough to sneak up on anyone. We just kind of hung in the sky like a big fat slow-moving target.

We were just a kilometer outside a small hamlet when I spotted a group of about thirty people below us who appeared to be moving down the road in military formation. They were all carrying what looked like some kind of weapon on their shoulders. There also was a man in the front who seemed to be acting as a leader for the group. They were all dressed in the typical black pajamas that the Viet Cong (and most everyone living in Nam) wore. Since this was so close to the Ho Chi Minh Trail, it certainly appeared that it could be a squad of VC.

The major went into action right away giving orders. He immediately decided they were VC troops—he had no doubts. He ordered me to fire my M-60 machine gun on the formation below. Now an M-60 can fire 750 rounds a minute and would have shredded that group in just a few seconds. I looked down at the formation, but then I froze. I couldn't pull the trigger. I could not get myself to squeeze off a single round. I was overcome with a feeling that something wasn't right.

I sat behind my M-60, doing nothing. The major was going crazy and yelling at me that he had given me a direct order to fire. It was not optional. But I just sat there, knowing that something was wrong with this picture. I told the major I was not going to fire. I had some heavy doubts about what we were seeing down on the road.

The major could not believe that I had actually questioned his orders. He was mad as hell. He told me that I had disobeyed a direct order in combat—a punishable offense. He let me know in no uncertain terms that he was going to bring me up on charges. Those charges could mean twenty years or more in a military prison at Leavenworth.

I told him we needed to fly lower so we could get a better identification. In the meantime, he had circled the aircraft so that the left door gunner was directly in line to fire his weapon. To my surprise, the door gunner also refused to shoot, showing exceptional courage by supporting my position. He fully understood what he had just done, and that took my breath away. He was certainly not looking for any trouble from the major, but there he was making a stand with me on this issue. It could have been viewed as a mutiny by the military court system. This was a serious breach of military law, and we each could have been facing life sentences. I was in awe that he had such courage and conviction, all based on his belief in my feelings. I hoped to God I was right, for both of our futures.

The major was debating with the copilot about calling in an air strike or at least some artillery. The young pilot, who had flown with us many times before, suggested we take the aircraft down for a closer look. Finally, after what seemed a very long time (even though it was less than a minute), we dropped down from our rather awkward altitude toward the group of people on the ground. We had our M-60 machine guns at the ready position, aimed right at the heart of the group.

We came down to about 100 feet, unsure of what to expect and ready for all hell to break loose as we passed to the right of them. The first clue that they might not be the enemy was the fact that they stayed on the road the whole time we were above them. They had not run into the cover of the surrounding jungle. The second big clue was that no one was firing at us.

As we flew across the road, it became painfully obvious to all of us who they were: just a group of school children with their garden tools, marching in a formation to the community garden. The leader was a priest dressed all in black. My heart raced; I got all emotional and felt tears rolling down my face, realizing just how close we had come to killing all these children.

I couldn't see the major's face, but I imagine it turned pale. All of us were visibly shaken. The major had given direct orders to both his gunners to kill them all. He even wanted to order an air strike on this group of children. Now he said very little.

Why had I, and my trusting door gunner, refused to fire? I have no answers. I went with my feelings, which were very clear and strong that I should not pull the trigger. I risked going to jail because I followed my feelings and not my orders.

I quickly learned never to question my intuitive feelings in Nam. It seemed that those feelings were greatly heightened in combat and dangerous situations. In this case, it saved children and a priest. I could never have lived with that; it would have haunted me the rest of my life.

After that day, the major and I became friends. He began to ask questions and rely on the combat-experienced men around him. He learned to trust those working for him. He turned out to be a very good human being and a fine officer. He also proved many times over to be a brave and courageous pilot—someone I felt confident flying with and risking my own life for. I think we both learned something that day that forever changed the way we looked at life and ourselves.

Bill McDonald

Bill McDonald is an author, poet, artist, minister, documentary filmmaker, veterans advocate, and the founder and past president of Military Writers Society of America. A crew chief/door gunner on Huey helicopters in 1966 and 1967, Bill flew with the 128th Helicopter Assault Company out of Phu Loi, South Vietnam. He was awarded the Distinguished Flying Cross, the Bronze Star Medal, fourteen Air Medals, the Purple Heart, and other medals and awards.

Like most who encounter the moral extremes of combat, Bill discovered that war is a crucible of spiritual transformation, impossible to live through without being changed. To understand his own experiences, Bill began to write about them and discovered hundreds of other warriors driven to explore and reveal their experiences. Bill's vision to bring them together led to the creation of MWSA.

After retiring, Bill went back to Vietnam in 2002 to help build a bridge of peace with his former enemies. He wrote about that experience in 2003 in his first book, *A Spiritual Warrior's Journey.* His acclaimed poetry book *Purple Hearts* was published in 2004, followed by his award-winning poetry book *Sacred Eye: Poetry in Search of the Divine.*

Bill is still married to his high school sweetheart and has two grown children and three grandchildren.

19

IN ONE'S WEAKNESS...

Barbara Perkins-Brown

It was summer, but the nights seemed cooler than ever. He woke up in the middle of the night in a frantic state—an abnormal condition that gradually seemed normal to him since this was not the first time he experienced this. Distraught by the same dream for almost two years now, his body was shaken and his back was covered by droplets of chilly sweats, and the same old familiar feeling of fear and horror was not all that easy to get used to. The images dwelled constantly inside his head, no matter how hard he tried to shut them off from his memory—the dark gray smoke from the aftermath of seemingly endless bombing and gunfire, the oozing thick and silky blood scattered on the ground, and the heavy stench of blown-up limbs in slow decay. They were haunting him. He felt powerless, yet he didn't want to be defeated.

He was once a revered officer in the military. He gave commands and orders. His uniform was well-decorated with medals and honors; almost everyone who had heard of his exceptional leadership could not help but admire his valor. He was in Operation Desert Shield during his early years in the service, and later on he successfully rose to the rank of a major. He then deployed to Iraq, where he was shot multiple times, but miraculously survived. However, four of his men did not make it when their Humvee hit a mine and burst into flames. This did not fatally hurt them, but the sudden array of flying bullets coming from several unknown directions took the lives of his men until silence dominated the darkness. He was covered with blood. Slowly he lost consciousness. That was the last scenario he could vividly recall after he woke up in the hospital in Balad. Apparently, he and his men were left for dead in the ambush. A couple of days later, they were found by the search and rescue troop.

He could not count how many times he had told himself that he was willing to serve his countrymen even in the face of death. Now the recollection of those men who died under his watch dwarfed that noble desire. He would have been better off if he died with them—the thought that kept on nagging his conscience. He thought he was a tough guy, only to prove himself wrong when in that very moment death was staring him in the face, he was not that tough at all. He called himself a coward. He blamed himself countless times. Reality called him out. He was a military hero for many, but that idea was far from the truth, and in that fateful night, the combat zone proved his point. He had too many unanswered questions. Why did he not take action the way he imagined he would and the way he was trained he should? Now he had doubt hanging over his head about his true self—the perception he had of himself was totally in contradiction with the person he actually was. Who could help him figure this out or at least help him address those questions he was desperately seeking answers for?

Where is his freedom from all of this? Freedom is safeguarded by the men and women in uniform. It has become a cliché to repeat the statement, "Freedom is not free," and many have not realized that there's sacredness in that proverbial line. Life has been sacrificed, and those who were able to come home have to live their lives in the realm of an altered reality.

He was diagnosed with post traumatic stress disorder and gradually understood that he was in conflict with himself because of the trauma he had suffered in the combat zone. The courage to face one's demon allows one's action to tap on hope. He now knew the face of hope that seemed unrecognizable in the battlefield, but he was given the reassurance that hope was always and ever present in everyone's life. Hope is like a fresh breath of freedom from anything that can hold a person captive—physical, mental, or spiritual. Hope allows one to believe that help is on the way.

At first he didn't know how to handle his situation; as if it was unconquerable, but his struggle was not only psychological but also spiritual. He was ashamed and in denial. But his family, church, and the chaplain, as well as the medical professionals at the VA hospital, provided assistance needed for his healing, such as prayers and encouragement. The chaplain and his church led him to his spiritual awakening—forgiving himself and accepting the fact that there was nothing he could have done to save his men. He only survived because the rescue came in time. He was able to live because of his comrades—they were his physical saviors.

The courage to accept one's limitations is hope in motion, acknowledging the fact that one has to lean on someone greater and more powerful. Finally, the most remarkable thing had happened to him, the knowledge of having a spiritual savior.

It was not an overnight success, but a gradual process that he found Jesus in his life and surrendered all his nightmares, fears, and distress to Him. Healing is the freedom from any sorts of illness, including PTSD. Christ has a transformational healing power, making hope and courage as one of the prescription pills. The courage to keep on living regardless of one's past gives hope to spiritual renewal.

His painful experience was real, and his needs were, too. Jesus became real to him, and the Scripture assured him: My grace is sufficient for thee: for my strength is made perfect in weakness. Most gladly therefore will I rather glory in my infirmities, that the power of Christ may rest upon me. (II Corinthians 12:9)

Barbara Perkins-Brown

Barbara Perkins-Brown, Ed.D., is a public educator with twelve years of secondary education experience teaching high school English and advanced placement courses. In 2009, she earned her doctorate in Educational Leadership, Policy, and Law from Alabama State University.

Barbara served in the Army National Guard from 1997 to 2004 as a specialist. While in boot camp, she was awarded Soldier of the Week and was a distinguished honor graduate from the Adjutant General School in Fort Jackson, South Carolina. She also received the Army Achievement Medal.

At age thirteen, Barbara started writing and has not stopped since. Her book, *Subic: A Sailor's Memoir Based on the Story of Bobby Earl Perkins,* unveils a little-known, but historically relevant, account of her father and his fellow servicemen who endured racial discrimination in the military while stationed in Subic Bay Naval Base, Philippines, during the late 1960s.

Barbara loves writing poetry and devotional guides to profess her Christian faith. Some of her works include *54 Poems for the Lord in 2 Days, Sackcloth: Voices in Verse, The Joys Within,* and *In the Presence of the Ultimate: A Guide to Spiritual Inquiry.* An active part of Alabama State Poetry Society, Alabama Writers Conclave, Military Writers Society of America, A Galaxy of Verse, and Toastmasters International, Barbara lives in Montgomery, Alabama, enjoying the Southern lifestyle with her four children.

20

SUSQUEHANNA SERVICE DOGS OPENING DOORS, SAVING LIVES

Don Helin

It's a little after nine o'clock on Thursday morning and SSD (Susquehanna Service Dog) Bridge, along with seven of his mates, is being loaded into a van to go to the mall. Not for a "shop till you drop" excursion, but rather a training expedition.

Amanda Nicholson is the training coordinator for Susquehanna Service Dogs. "Each Tuesday and Thursday, we transport the dogs to malls around the area for training on how to behave among distractions such as other people, shopping carts, and so forth. These dogs," Nicholson continues, "are permitted by law to travel with and help their partners inside crowded areas, and they must be trained, and then tested periodically, to prove they are able to do that."

My wife and I are volunteer trainers with SSD. At the mall, we work with the dogs to practice the various commands the dogs have already learned from their puppy raisers—sit, stand, stay, come, heel, retrieve—then help them learn the advanced tasks they must know to support their potential partners.

These more advanced tasks include visit (putting his chin on his partner's knee to calm him in the event of a meltdown), take it (picking up a leash or something else his partner may have dropped on the floor and can't reach), and about twenty other commands which will be of value to his partner.

During this time period, we take our dog for the day to a food court to train the dog to practice lying quietly under a table while we may be having lunch or a cup of tea. "Down stays" of thirty minutes or more are required. It's critical that SSD Bridge pays attention to his trainer and no one else. Later, his partner's safety may depend on it.

Only Young Once

SSD Bridge began his career on September 12, 2013, snuggled with other puppies and his mom. Each litter receives a name. For example, Bridge is from the city litter. At approximately eight weeks, he left the friendly environs of the litter to spend a week in the kennel for a physical and other health checks, then moved to the next step in his training: life with a puppy raiser.

SSD Bridge lived with his puppy raiser in State College, Pennsylvania, from eight weeks to approximately eighteen months and learned not only basic commands, but also how to control the urges that most dogs live out every day—running, barking, playing. SSD Bridge must be given time to be a dog, but at the same time, as a service dog in training, he learned the skills and behavior he will require. At eighteen months, SSD Bridge moved into the kennel with other dogs his age to begin learning the advanced skills needed of service dogs. Here is where my wife and I and other volunteer trainers come in.

Meet the Dogs

After three months in the kennel working with his trainers to improve his skills, SSD Bridge, along with three or four other service dogs in training, will meet potential partners. It may be a soldier with post traumatic stress disorder, a woman in a wheelchair, a child with autism, or a man with multiple sclerosis. The potential partners greet and play with each of the dogs. Then decisions are made about which dog will best fit the needs of which partner. Every partner is special, and each dog must be carefully matched to meet the needs of that partner. For example, it takes a relatively large, strong dog to pull a wheelchair or act as a balance dog.

Once SSD Bridge is matched with a partner, he will spend the next three months learning the specific skills required by his new partner. At approximately twenty-three months, SSD Bridge and his partner will spend three weeks working together with trainers, polishing the skills the partnership will use.

In SSD Bridge's case, he is programmed to become a balance dog. If that's the final decision, SSD Bridge must be trained to carry the special balance harness with a U-shaped metal rod on his back that his partner will be able to grab onto it whenever he feels unsteady. After the three week training period, the partnership will be tested to make sure they work well together, and have both learned the skills required to be able to move around the community and support one another.

Susquehanna Service Dogs has placed approximately 250 service dogs that provide needed assistance to their partners on a daily basis. Each of these dogs has a special story about how they have helped their partner.

For example, we placed a service dog with an 11-year-old girl with a significant psychiatric illness and autism. The girl's family had tried many other support services with little success. Nothing helped until SSD Hamlet came into their lives.

At the time, the girl was a D/F student in school, with few friends and many meltdowns, according to her mother. Hamlet had an immediate positive effect. Together the family taught the dog to exert full body pressure which provides a significant calming effect. Immediately the girl's meltdowns decreased in duration and slowly decreased in frequency. And her grades improved dramatically. That girl's life has changed markedly for the better because of her service dog.

There are a myriad of success stories as to what these wonderful dogs can do. I particularly enjoy working with our veterans, many of whom have serious cases of post traumatic stress. Chris had spent two tours in Iraq and one in Afghanistan. I vividly remember one day when I came out of the side door of a mall with Chris. He glanced over at another store and told me, "That's where the sniper would be." Chris spends his life looking for snipers who may try to harm him.

Three weeks after Chris and his service dog completed their training together, we received an email from him. "For the first time in the past four years," Chris said, "I feel like I want to get up in the morning. I need to take care of my best friend, SSD Sammi."

Stories like that of hope and courage are what make all the work of training these wonderful dogs worthwhile.

Don Helin

Don Helin grew up in Minneapolis and attended the University of Minnesota through the ROTC program. Upon graduation, he entered the Army, serving three tours in the Pentagon, multiple tours overseas including Germany and Vietnam, and various posts in the United States. After he left the Army, he worked as a lobbyist for the chemical industry. These two careers taught him that, indeed, truth is stranger than fiction and together have provided more than enough material for his thriller novels. Don spent four years as a travel writer before turning to writing fiction. His articles have been published in numerous newspapers and magazines.

Using his experience from the military, including eight years in the Pentagon, Don published his first thriller, *Thy Kingdom Come*, in 2009. It tells the story of a group of white supremacists stealing nuclear material to make dirty bombs. His second, *Devil's Den*, was selected as a finalist in the Indie Book Awards. His most recent thriller, *Secret Assault*, was published this past November.

Don is an active member of International Thriller Writers, Mystery Writers of America, Military Writers Society of America, and Pennwriters, a statewide writer's group in Pennsylvania. He is also a mentor with Mystery Writers of America. He and his wife, along with their cute little Cockapoo, live in central Pennsylvania outside of Harrisburg where he is hard at work on his next Zack Kelly thriller, *Dark Angel*.

21

SAVED TO SERVE

Tom Gauthier

Of the 367 men who went to war, 356 came home, each with a Purple Heart Medal. Their mission was a secret then and little known today. But how do you write a history of a World War II military unit when the official records of that unit lie at the bottom of the Pacific Ocean? The answer involves some serendipity, some luck, and the tenacity of one man to rebuild the story of his and his comrades' war experiences. This group of men organized for a unique mission of a World War II Pacific Campaign.

A memorial plaque at Wright-Patterson Air Force Base reads: "Initially torpedoed and almost destroyed, the squadron rose from disaster to top performance of its control mission in the air war of the Pacific."

The unit was activated on 13 January 1942 at Selfridge Field, Michigan. After training, the unit was ordered to March Field, Riverside, California. Arriving by troop train, they proceeded by truck to the Los Angeles Air Defense Wing. Designated the 1st Fighter Control Squadron (Sep), they began building and training the organization into its unique new mission.

The squadron had its roots in the systems developed by the British to defend against German air assaults. British centers remained fixed along the coast, warning of German aircraft, and guiding the RAF to intercept. By contrast, the

1st Fighter Control Squadron landed on beachheads, fought their way inland, and established control centers as quickly as possible, defending the area against Japanese air attacks, guiding American fighter planes to intercept incoming enemy planes. They provided homing communications for lost pilots, and guidance for air-sea rescue.

Members of the 1st Fighters had a system that was one of the best kept secrets of the war. Neither Nazi Germany nor the Japanese ever learned why we were so successful in detecting aircraft, giving early warnings, and intercepting them both day and night.

By 1943, fully trained, systems proven, 367 men sailed aboard the troopship SS Cape San Juan, along with other Army units totaling 1,464 men. In the early morning of 11 November 1943, their ship steamed on a westerly course, 300 miles southeast of Fiji. The weather was clear, seas choppy with whitecaps, the sun not yet risen but light enough to see clearly, as the 2nd mate stood morning watch. Blacked out and zigzagging with lookouts at general quarters, the Cape San Juan was executing a turn to starboard when torpedo wakes were spotted. Within seconds she was hit by a torpedo fired by a Japanese submarine.

Accounts of that day tell of lost lives, but the fact that more than 1,000 men entered the shark-infested, rain-swept seas that morning and all but 117 made it out, is nothing short of a miracle. A miracle of men selflessly putting their own lives at risk to help others in the cold water, encouraging their buddies to "hold on just a little longer."

The first rescue ship, Edwin T. Meredith, arrived five hours later, circling the area and picking up survivors. Several of her seamen exhibited extreme courage by diving into the shark-infested, oil-covered waters to pull exhausted men to safety. The chief mate described the scene of horror he found when his ship reached the scene: "Sharks tore bodies from partially submerged life rafts. Some of the sharks had already made off with screaming men, and the blood from the bodies of those boys attracted more sharks—even pulling men off rafts."

The 1st Fighter Control Squadron lost ten men that day. One additional man was killed later in a kamikaze attack. The entire organization suffered exposure to the elements, fuel oil to the eyes, and various broken bones and lacerations. The men were hospitalized and treated, but eventually gathered in Brisbane, Australia, to continue their mission.

Their first action: the invasion of Hollandia. The 1st Fighter Control Squadron Detachment A, led by Lieutenant Edward Bonfoey, went ashore with the first wave of infantry in the Humboldt Bay segment of the Hollandia Operation. Bonfoey quickly established the facility for early enemy air raid warning, controlling anti-aircraft fire and Navy and Air Corps fighter planes. This was the mission of the 1st Fighter Control Squadron, built on long training, innovation, and survival at sea.

The next combat landing for them was Wakde Island. Fighting still raged when they moved forward to Insoemanai Island. The soldiers located missing aircraft, effected rescues, steered lost planes to bases, issued code messages for air strikes, provided weather information, and maintained 24-hour alert for defending aircraft.

Sailing for the next combat landing at Leyte/Mindoro, they reported, "We were under suicide attacks by the Japs, terrified to see those planes dive straight at a ship. One plane headed for our LST, but continuous fire by guns shot it down a short distance from us. One ship behind us was hit and sank immediately. We were lucky—the good Lord was on our side once again!"

In December of 1944, two U.S. 7th Fleet task groups sailed for Mindoro, Philippines. Many enemy aircraft were destroyed by escorting U.S. planes and Navy gunfire. A diary note from a 1st Fighter recorded, "In short intervals, Jap planes would burst into flames and plummet into the ocean...vivid memory of fanatical Kamikaze pilots diving their planes steeply to crash into our vessels...terrific explosions resulted, followed by flames gutting the ship...great loss of life."

Several days later they reached Mindoro. After a preliminary beachhead bombardment, troops landed south of Luzon. Captain Bonfoey's detachment landed on Blue Beach. During the night, air raids had men tumbling into foxholes and finding themselves submerged in sea water from the rising tide.

Another mission followed. In July of 1945, after some weather delays, the 1st Fighters flew to new control center locations on Laoag and Lingayan, Philippines.

In August of 1945, the first atomic bombs were dropped on Hiroshima and Nagasaki, followed by Japan's surrender. But the war for the 1st Fighters was still on, spotting stray enemy aircraft, while missions to locate crippled allied aircraft continued.

The next month, Purple Heart Medals were awarded to the 1st Fighters injured during the torpedoing disaster. Shortly thereafter, the "Swan Song" for the 1st Fighters was finally played. That last month of 1945, four long years after the attack on Pearl Harbor, was the last for the 1st Fighter Control Squadron as a World War II organization.

After serving with skill and honor through the New Guinea and Philippines campaigns—and having established itself as the last operational fighter control squadron in the Philippines— the 1st Fighter Control Squadron was finally "put on the shelf" for a well-deserved rest.

RIP, Brothers.

[Excerpted from *The Saga of the 1ˢᵗ Fighter Control Squadron: Memories of Our History, 2015*]

Thomas D. Gauthier

Dr. Tom Gauthier is published on various subjects in newspapers, national and international journals, and has authored, produced, and directed four plays. His first novel, *Code Name: Orion's Eye*, has become something of a cult favorite with World War II veterans and their families, especially those who fought in the South Pacific. It was the first in his Amos Mead Adventures, now continuing in five more novels: *Mead's Trek, Die Liste: Revenge on the Black Sun, Force Three Rises*, and the soon to be released, *The President's Deadly Enemy*. He received a "Notable Award for Literary Fiction" in an International Writer's Digest Book Award competition.

Born in 1940 in California, growing up in Santa Barbara, Tom served in the U.S. Army as a combat intelligence analyst and the Air Force Reserve as a Loadmaster on a C-119. His civilian career took him to every corner of North America and twenty countries. Holding a BS/Management, an M.B.A., and an master's and doctorate in psychology, Tom is a member of Delta Epsilon Tau, an international honors society. He is a private pilot, a member of the Elks Lodge, and the American Legion. In retirement, his primary focus is writing novels, but he continues to consult with companies and governments on organizational and communications issues.

Tom and his wife of forty years, Marlene, built their dream home on a small ranch in the Eastern Sierras and enjoy the visits of thirteen grandchildren and seventeen great-grandchildren.

22

FACING FEARS

Valerie Ormond

Sadie arrived at Fort Belvoir wiping her clammy hands on her pants. Captain Vinson greeted her again, this time for the final visit of her internship with the Caisson Platoon Equine Assisted Program.

"So here's the plan. You're going to help me do my job today at the grooming station." He brought her out to the same grooming station as the last time, several large wooden poles anchored in a sand footing. "Help where you're needed and be yourself. I'll go get the horses and today you'll get to meet our veteran riders."

* * *

Captain Vinson returned with a horse, along with a young woman, dark hair pulled back in a braid. Strangely, Sadie thought, this woman could be an older version of herself.

"Sergeant Marie Silva, this is Sadie Navarro, the one I told you about," Captain Vinson said. Sadie wondered what he had told her. Sergeant Silva did not have full use of the left side of her body. Or, correction, from what Sadie had learned, Sergeant Silva *could* use the right side of her body, and had *some* use of the left side of her body.

"It's nice to meet you, Sadie. If you're ready to get to work, you can help me clean up Ben."

Sergeant Silva grabbed the currycomb out of the tack box and began working the large gray draft gelding. The gray arched his neck away from her in an invitation to rub there more. "I love this guy. Ben thinks he's a big dog. He's one of my favorites."

"So, you've been coming here for a while?"

"Yes, it's been very helpful. I've gained a lot of strength and balance. And these guys," she patted Ben with her stiffer left hand, "have a way of connecting with the soul like no other animals."

"I know. I love horses," Sadie offered, while brushing the dirt off the huge gray legs with a hard grooming brush.

"Can I answer any questions for you about the horses and what happens here?"

"Well, yes, if you don't mind. You see, I've had a chance to learn about therapeutic riding at one place, and how it helps children with autism. And I'm volunteering at another place, where I'm learning how horses help kids learn responsibility. And am I already talking too much?"

"No, please go on. I enjoy your enthusiasm." Sergeant Silva now maneuvered Ben's first hoof into position to pick it out. She caught Sadie watching, and said, "Go on; I'm fine. I'm interested in your question."

"Would you mind telling me your opinion of what's best about this program?"

"Excellent question and an easy answer. But now you'll have to tell me if I'm talking too much. It's an easy answer, but not a short one." She took a breath and moved on to Ben's next hoof.

"I had a successful Army career and everything going for me. When I got injured in Iraq, everything changed. I went through a rough time where I felt depressed and worthless, and even suicidal. I lost hope."

Sadie filled the quiet space, now regretting she had asked the stupid question. "Can I help with the last two hooves?"

"If you must. But it's not because I need the help."

"I understand. But you're working and talking, and I'm standing here when I'm supposed to be helping."

"Fair enough. So, where was I? Oh, I met Mary Jo out at the Walter Reed Medical Center, and she invited me to take part in the program. She sensed I needed help. While I've made great strides physically, it has been the emotional healing that's been strongest. I see my Army brethren here; I'm on a base; I'm still part of the team. We cheer each other on and celebrate our successes. It's the camaraderie and the fact of knowing that so many people care about what happens to us. That's what separates this program from the rest.

"After hitting bottom, this place gave me confidence. Now I know nothing can stop me, not even a bomb. I may do things a different way, but if I set my mind to something, I can do it. Does that answer your question?"

Sadie hesitated to answer, soaking it in. Now she was glad she had asked the question. "Sure does, Sergeant, and thank you for everything—your answer, your service, and your honesty. I really appreciate it. I could never learn all this from a book."

"Just in time, here's the captain. Don't you love him? He's like Ben, one of my favorites. He tries to be all tough on the outside, but on the inside he's a marshmallow."

"I recognize your look there, Sergeant. You'd better not be telling our future volunteer stories about me. She may not come back."

"Oh, she'll be back. Trust me. If she sets her mind to something, she will do it." The sergeant winked at Sadie.

"No doubt," he answered. "Sadie, why don't you come on over with us? Our job here at the grooming station is done for the day, but you can observe Sergeant Silva's riding session if you'd like to. She already agreed."

"Thank you. I'd love to, and I won't even offer to help." The two girls exchanged a knowing grin.

Sadie stood at the fence with Captain Vinson, watching the horse and rider team. The Army soldier side-walker moved alongside without interfering. Sergeant Silva directed Ben where she wanted him to go. She used a combination of her hips and the single-handed rein holder Mary Jo showed Sadie on day one, so long ago. After the sergeant weaved in and out of a series of lined up poles, she brought Ben to a perfect square halt. Everyone cheered, and Sadie cheered the loudest.

Sadie had never met such brave people. They didn't want anyone to feel sorry for them, and they didn't want anyone to do things for them. She comprehended the theme: they weren't *disabled*, just *differently-abled*. Their strength empowered Sadie and she wanted to move from the past into the present and let go of worries polluting her mind. These brave souls led her from the darkness to a new light.

At the end of the session, Captain Vinson walked Sadie to her family's car. Sadie waited a moment, and found her courage. "Captain, before I go, I have a confession to make. I was scared to death to work with the veterans. With my dad still gone and with everything else...I don't know. I'm sorry, it scared me."

"I know, Sadie. It's why I wanted you to do it. Thank you for facing your fears. I hope you feel better now."

The gruff old teddy bear gave her a warm hug and patted her on the back. The people Sadie had feared most had taught her lessons of a lifetime.

[Excerpted from *Believing In Horses, Too* (2014)]

Valerie Ormond

Valerie Ormond retired as a Navy captain intelligence officer and was one of the first women to serve on combat aircraft carriers. In her final assignments, she directed efforts of a 500-person organization supporting global operations, coordinated executive level briefing, and writing support to the offices of the Joint Chiefs of Staff and Secretary of Defense, and managed policy and programs for 23,000 naval intelligence personnel.

In 2014, Valerie participated in Syracuse University's Veteran Women Igniting the Spirit of Entrepreneurship (V-WISE) program and founded Veteran Writing Services, LLC. Her business provides professional writing and consulting services, and clients have included large and small businesses, non-profit organizations, and individuals.

Valerie's two novels, *Believing in Horses* and *Believing In Horses, Too*, both won gold medals from Military Writers Society of America. Numerous books and magazines feature her nonfiction stories. A member of the National Women Veterans Speakers Bureau, she also speaks to audiences sharing lessons learned.

Her education includes a Master of Strategic Studies from the U.S. Army War College; a Master of Strategic Intelligence from the Defense Intelligence College; and a bachelor of arts in English and Mass Communication from Towson University. She belongs to numerous military and veterans' organizations and serves as secretary of the Maryland Horse Council, a trade organization representing 30,000 people in the horse industry.

Valerie lives with her husband Jaime Navarro, in Bowie, Maryland, where they enjoy the company of their wonderful families and friends, their three horses, and four dogs.

23

GOTTA BELIEVE 'FORE YOU CAN DO

Carolyn P. Schriber

"Teaching these slave women to read is rather like teaching a parrot to recite his ABCs. He can do it, if he's clever, but you don't believe for a moment that he knows what a B is."

"What you're seeing, I think, is another part of the slave mentality that we are all just beginning to understand."

"They are not congenitally stupid, Laura. I refuse to believe that."

"No, and that is not what I meant. Not understanding is a survival skill. Imagine for a moment that you are a slave. Your master tells you to muck out the entire stable, but it is nearly dark and turning cold. If you refuse to do it, you'll be beaten, perhaps severely. So you go out and sweep up the area just on either side of the door. Then, when the master berates you for not completing the job, you can say, 'Sorry, massa. I dint unnerstan.' You're still in trouble, but you're probably not going to be beaten and sold for disobedience."

"How do we overcome that attitude?"

"I'm not sure, Ellen. Perhaps when these people fully realize that they are free, they will feel more of the need for education. Right now, they're still very confused about their status, as well they should be. They know their masters could still come back to claim them. And if the owners return, they are not going to be happy to find educated slaves. The slaves know that, so they have little reason to make progress beyond the simplest things we ask."

"Then why do we . . .?"

"Because we can't do anything else. Someone has to try to get through to them. We can't predict their futures, but we can try to make them better."

***

Ellen puzzled over the problem for several days before she broached the discussion again. "I have an idea. Would there be any objection to my starting a class just for adults here at the house? We could use that back corner room, where the cotton agent stored his supplies."

"I don't see a problem with that, so long as it doesn't make you sneeze. The room is still full of cotton fluff. But how will it be any different from what the other schools are doing?"

"For starters, there would be no children tagging along. I don't want the women distracted. Then I'm going to ask them to write first and learn to read later."

"I can't imagine what you mean. Sounds impossible."

"Not really. It's an attempt to overcome that obstacle we discussed the other day—the lack of a reason to learn."

"I still don't follow."

"Let me give you an example. Call Rina in here, would you?"

When Rina arrived, looking puzzled, Ellen invited her to sit down. The former slave still looked the part, head bowed so as not to make eye contact, hands hidden by her apron, one foot twisted around the other ankle.

"Relax, Rina. You're on a break from your chores. Have a seat."

"Duz you mean me? I aint sposed fuh sit in de house."

"I'm giving you permission, Rina," Laura said from the corner, where she had settled herself to observe.

"No, tankee, Ma'am. I be gwine stan."

Ellen took out a small pad of paper. "Can you read and write, Rina?" she asked.

"No'm. I aint neber larned dat."

"Well, if you could write something—a sign, maybe—what would you like it to say?"

Rina shook her head. "I don unnerstan what you be wantin me fuh do."

"A sign, Rina. I'm going to make you a sign. A sign you can put anywhere to tell other people what to do. What do you want it to say?"

"Ain't neber hab no sign," Rina protested.

"Now you're going to have one. It will be Rina's sign. What should it say?"

"I kin puts it ennywheres?"

"Yes."

"Den, maybe it be sayin sumptin bout muh chikkuns?"

"If that's what you want, yes."

"Den make it say, 'Dese be Rina's chikkuns. Leave dem be."

Ellen tried very hard not to laugh as she wrote down Rina's words: THESE BE RINA'S CHICKENS. LEAVE THEM BE.

"Dat what dose marks mean? Dat be writin?"

"Yes. That's what we mean by writing."

"An I kin takes dat sign an puts it on muh chikkun coop?"

"That's the idea."

"An dose lil marks gwine protect muh chikkuns?"

"I can't promise you that a dog won't get your chickens, since dogs can't read. But soldiers surely can read. If soldiers have been stealing your chickens, then this sign should keep them away."

"It kinda like magic, den?" Rina's eyes were wide with excitement.

"It is a kind of magic. It makes you very powerful." Ellen nodded toward Laura. "The ability to read and write is what gives women like Miss Laura her power to run this plantation."

"Kin ennybody do dat?"

"Anybody can learn how to write, yes."

"Den I wants fuh larn it. An kin we larn how fuh write udder tings, too?"

"Of course. Do you want another sign?"

"I wuz tinkin dat ol Bess mebbe like a sign fuh she taters."

"I can do that." Ellen took out another piece of paper and wrote: THESE BE BESS'S POTATOES. LEAVE THEM BE.

"What dat sign say?"

"It says, 'These be Bess's potatoes. Leave them be'."

"Jis like what muh sign say. Kin I sees dose?" Rina put the two sheets of paper on the table next to one another, and her eyes flashed back and forth between them. Ellen and Laura were both holding their breath.

Finally, Rina spoke. "Dese be Rina's chikkuns. Dese be Bess's taters. Dat word dere. Dat be muh name? An dat one be Bess's name?"

"You're reading them, Rina!" Laura said, her eyes stinging from the effort to hold back her tears.

"Yes'm. Make me annudduh sign."

This time, Ellen did not ask. She simply wrote out two more sentences: THESE BE JOE'S SHOES. LEAVE THEM BE.

"What dat word?"

"Joe."

"An what dat word?"

"Shoes."

"Dat sign, it say, 'Dese be Joe's shoes. Leave dem be'."

"That's right."

"Lawd uh mercy! I kin read?"

"Yes, you can read a little bit. And you can learn to read much more than just these signs."

"Kin I larn fuh make dem marks?"

"Certainly. That's called learning your ABCs. Some of the women have been already studying those. Would you like to have your own class?"

"Missus Laura? She be teasin me?" She looked at Laura for permission to believe the impossible.

"No, Rina. She's not teasing. If you and Susannah and the others would like to go to school, you can have some time off every afternoon to meet here with Miss Ellen. She will be your teacher. And I promise you, she's a good one."

[Excerpted from *The Road to Frogmore: Turning Slaves into Citizens* (Katzenhaus Books, 2012)]

Carolyn Schriber

Carolyn Schriber hated history classes when she was growing up because they required little but memorization. Once she was so bored by the material that instead of answering an essay exam on the Revolutionary War, she filled in the space by writing several verses of "The Star-Spangled Banner." The professor gave her an A, which may have suggested that he was as tired of names and dates as she was. Or maybe he was just impressed that she knew more than the first verse.

Eventually, however, she discovered a teacher who was an enthusiastic storyteller, and her love of history blossomed. She went on to earn her doctoral degree in medieval history and America's Civil War and spent the last seventeen years of her teaching career as a college professor.

After retirement from Rhodes College, Schriber used her great-uncle's letters to analyze the Battle of Secessionville (*A Scratch with the Rebels*, 2007). Next she examined the life of a nurse who was present at that battle (*Beyond All Price*, 2010) and wrote a biography of a missionary who arrived to care for abandoned slaves (*The Road to Frogmore*, 2012). Most recently she has been writing about civilians whose lives were forever disrupted by these events (*Left by the Side of the Road*, 2012, and *Damned Yankee*, 2014). Two of her Civil War books have received medals from the Military Writers Society of America—a bronze medal for *Beyond All Price* and a silver medal for *The Road to Frogmore*.

Mammy Prater, 115-year-old ex-slave.
Photo from the Library of Congress Archives

24

SHE'S COME UNDONE

Kathleen Rodgers

I wrote this a few months after my dad and my dog died, five days apart. I'd also just completed my second novel, *Johnnie Come Lately*, and I was struggling to find a literary agent to represent my work. The novel is a midlife coming of age about a woman named Johnnie Kitchen and her search for self-fulfillment and forgiveness. Like Johnnie, I was also a military mom facing the reality of sending a son to war. Both the poem and the novel deal with a woman who is learning to let go of matters out of her control. May others find hope and courage in my words.

Stepping out of the pool
wearing nothing but a dare,
she looks around.
No roofers in sight,
only the neighbor's cat
curled under the Mimosa
and a gecko doing pushups on the fence.
She crosses her arms in front of her
covering herself like a shield.
It's the Pilgrim in her, you know.
Then slowly, she drops the façade,
lifts her arms wide
and does breaststrokes in the air.

The stars aren't even out,
high noon howls at her back
as she glides this way and that,
barefoot in the sun,
pirouetting in grass that's still green
until the scarecrows come out.
A hawk flies overhead,
his high-pitched keeee calling her
to join him.
She takes off across the yard
and decades fall behind her,
shedding the years until she is five
and running through sprinklers.
Diving into the blue,
she torpedoes through the water
propelled by an energy
she hasn't felt in years.
When she comes up for air,
she spots two lily pads of cloth
floating nearby...the discarded suit.
Flipping on her back,
the buzz of a light plane catches her attention.
And she laughs at the moment
when she defied convention.

Kathleen Rodgers

Kathleen M. Rodgers is a former frequent contributor to *Family Circle Magazine* and *Military Times*. Her work has also appeared in anthologies published by McGraw-Hill, University of Nebraska Press/Potomac Books, Health Communications, Inc., AMG Publishers, and Press 53. She is the author of the 2009 MWSA Silver Medal Winner for her novel, *The Final Salute*, featured in *USA Today*, the Associated Press, and *Military Times*. Deer Hawk Publications reissued the novel in e-book and paperback September of 2014.

Her second novel, *Johnnie Come Lately*, released from Camel Press on February 1, 2015. The novel was spotlighted twice in Terri Barnes' popular column, "Spouse Calls," in *Stars & Stripes*. In 2014, Kathleen was named a Distinguished Alumna from Tarrant County College/NE Campus.

She is the mother of two grown sons, Thomas, a graduate of University of North Texas and a working artist in Denton, Texas, and J.P., a graduate of Texas Tech University and a former Army officer who earned a Bronze Star in 2014 in Afghanistan. Kathleen's husband, Tom, is a retired fighter pilot/commercial airline pilot, and they reside in Colleyville, Texas, with their rescue dog Denton. Kathleen is working on a new novel titled *Seven Wings to Glory* and is represented by Loiacono Literary Agency.

25

OF ALL PLACES

Duke Barrett

On a recent late and hot summer afternoon as I was driving home to Las Vegas from Los Angeles, I was visited by the gods, or ghosts (depending on one's political views, I suppose) of Southeast Asia, aka Vietnam. Where and how did this happen, you ask? Well, it wasn't in any tropical setting, rainforest, or ridiculous man-made greenbelt, but instead only a few miles west of Baker, California, home of the World's Tallest Thermometer, to be exact. Yes, you read that correctly, the World's Tallest Thermometer is smack-dab in the middle of the Mojave Desert.

Only minutes after whizzing by Zzyzx Road (yes, it too exists) on Interstate 15, I was taken back for a brief moment by an atmospherically induced condition. Now, excluding the extreme summer heat, this is one of the last places on earth that would remind me, or anyone who's ever been there, of Southeast Asia. But it did. Allow me to explain.

It had been raining off and on throughout the afternoon, and as a result, the normally parched desert valley floor had become, to put it mildly, moisture filled. Heading east as I descended into the valley, the sun somehow managed to work its magic as it strained to peek through openings in storm clouds, highlighting a fog that lifted toward the heavens and denied the surrounding hills of any clear definition. The unusual weather conditions had created a beautiful but surreal illusion of a mysterious wetland of rice paddies enhanced by the pouring rain on the rock-hard desert landscape.

Piloting my vehicle through the desert ever so carefully on the rain-slicked highway, I gazed to the horizon, looked back at the highway through my rearview mirror, and was again drawn to the horizon and approaching wet valley floor below. For a fleeting moment the once dry valley surface had taken on a look of tiny villages, sporadically inserted into a beautiful but hostile world of wet. I envisioned helicopters trading tracer rounds with an enemy below as the choppers circled above in support of friendly forces on the ground, all the while looking like a swarm of angry wasps.

Well aware of my geographical location, I couldn't help but be confused for that brief but intense moment, as I harkened back to my Army paratrooper days in the Central Highlands of South Vietnam, on the ground, in a hostile setting as part of said action.

"What the hell is going on?" I wondered. I like to think of myself as composed, but this incident had shaken my senses. Within seconds I regained my wits (which, by the way, came in handy at the legal speed limit) and continued my drive. I must have driven through Baker, both to and from Los Angeles, at least a couple hundred times over the years with nary a thought, but on this particular day, a Sunday, I said to myself, "Self, we gotta get out of this place."

Look, traumatic events leave no man unscathed and more often than not will leave a scar of some fashion, be it mental, physical, or both. I've never been one who's prone to flashbacks (or so I would like to believe), but there was no doubt I had been experiencing an involuntary conveyance to the past. Having said that, I must say that music has always had a profound effect on me, and at that particular point in time I had been listening to some classic R&B from back in the day on the radio. As an admitted part-time creature of moods, it so happened that I had my full creature on at that time and unbeknownst to me, fuel was being poured on an already flaming emotional fire. It was as if an oldies radio jock had personally asked me, "Do you remember where you were and what you were doing when this record was a hit?" Well, guess what? I do, and those memories have been forever ingrained into my being.

Every once in a while I need that proverbial swift kick to be reminded of all the good things life has rewarded me with, because I have a tendency, as many do, to allow life to become routine or humdrum. It was at that precise moment when I snapped out of my momentary trip to yesteryear and once again realized how novel and fulfilling my life actually is.

I've been blessed with a beautiful wife, children, grand-children, and a savings account, not to mention affordable healthcare, a Lexus, and an awesome cable TV package. I kid. It's safe to say I use sarcasm as a means to cope with the curveballs life occasionally throws my way. Can humor and levity be used as a legitimate coping mechanism? You bet! Both can be medicinal if we give them a chance, and I can attest to this by my forty-three years of marital bliss. Allow me to debunk the infamous myth that most of us combat veterans suffer from failed marriages due to post traumatic stress disorder, aka PTSD.

I will never deny having a number of physical and emotional confrontations with PTSD, but as of this writing, I'm ahead on points. I am still married to the same loving woman I met and fell in love with upon my return from foreign adventures. Over the years, like most married couples, we've had our share of life's ups and downs. We've laughed and cried and it certainly hasn't been all that easy. However, in spite of the difficulties we've managed to overcome a great number of her flaws. I kid, again; just ask my kids.

I do not believe anyone ever said life or marriage is easy, and if one did, that person is a fool. In many a memory dating back to my days in Southeast Asia and since, I've been able to put to rest the bad memories by realizing the folly of them for exactly what they are: folly.

Levity and laughter play a significant role in my life and marriage. Now, that's not to say that in any way, shape, or form, our marriage is akin to folly. As a matter of fact, I'd say that as we close in on our 44th wedding anniversary, we are on the verge of becoming a happily married couple, still crazy after all these years. Yes, crazy, and it doesn't get any better than that.

In conclusion, I'd say that on that hot wet summer afternoon I'd been served a "cocktail" of the elements and memories, mixed with music, emotions, and happenstance. Yes, passing through Baker, a normally precipitation-free environment, was indeed happenstance. This only serves to reinforce my thankfulness for life, love, family, and my insatiable craving of caustic-lite humor which facilitates my coping abilities.

I am also grateful for the fact that on that rainy day I was not on a perimeter of a hostile village in the Central Highlands of South Vietnam, but instead on the periphery of the desert town of Baker, California, of all places.

Duke Barrett

Duke Barrett is a combat veteran of the Vietnam War. The Chicago-born paratrooper served with the First Air Cavalry Division of the U.S. Army as both an infantryman and a reconnaissance scout. Upon completion of his tour in Vietnam, Duke was assigned to the 82nd Airborne Division at Fort Bragg, North Carolina. Duke is also the recipient of the Combat Infantryman's Badge and the Purple Heart Medal.

Upon completion of his military obligation, Duke resumed a musical career that had been interrupted by the draft. He has had the good fortune to have played every major nightclub and theater from coast to coast, to include Broadway's Alvin Theater in New York City where he played in the pit orchestra for the musical *Seven Brides for Seven Brothers* starring Debbie Boone. The one time rock 'n' roll drummer and former Golden Gloves champ still plays music on a part-time basis in Las Vegas and gets his kicks kicking a big band.

In 1970, Duke married the beautiful Mitsuko Hor, of Tokyo, Japan. They have three beautiful children: two sons and a daughter. They have also been blessed with two grandsons and one granddaughter.

A graduate of the University of Wisconsin Parkside with a degree in political science, Duke only recently retired from the U.S. Postal Service in Las Vegas, Nevada, following a 34-year career as a city letter carrier.

In 2007, Duke released his first novel, *The Wall of Broken Dreams*, and was honored to have had founder and former Military Writers Society president, W.H "Bill" McDonald, Jr., pen the book's foreword.

26

HOPE FOR THE LETTER H

Rob Ballister

As parents, we expect that in order to help our children thrive in society, we are going to have to teach them certain values: things like respect for authority, honor, and tolerance for others. I personally have always fully intended to teach my children that it doesn't matter what someone's skin color, personal religion, or sexual preference is; people are people and they need to be treated as such so the world can keep going 'round.

When my children were only six and not-quite-two, I hadn't yet gotten around to many of those lessons. It wasn't for lack of trying, but after almost six years of nothing but animated cartoons and large purple dinosaurs, my mind was pretty much fried. And I'm not really sure it would have mattered much anyway. My toddler son was still of the mind that all people, regardless of creed or color, existed for one purpose only, and that was to bring him juice. No matter the person's demeanor or appearance, within minutes of meeting them my son would approach the person and demand juice, usually channeling Nikita Khrushchev by banging his shoe on the table in the process. Of course, as he could say neither "juice" nor much of anything at that time, it mostly resulted in a lot of confusion and screaming. Occasionally, it resulted in head butting.

My daughter, much wiser at the age of six, didn't really seem to have a problem with different skin colors anyway (and also could get her own juice). We had a discussion that different people may have different skin, and that they may believe in different gods, and she seemed to accept that and went right on playing with her dolls and torturing the dog (we had yet to discuss canine equality).

So, imagine my surprise when one day she dropped a whopper of intolerance on me. We were lying in her bed as part of her bedtime ritual, which with my daughter began around six p.m. and stopped sometime about four minutes before dawn. We had already brushed her teeth, watched her TV show, said her prayers, checked for bugs, counted sheep, sung a song, and done all the other thousand things that had become part of the ritual, and finally she was getting ready to sleep. As I anxiously awaited her calm rhythmic breathing, which signaled I could escape and go watch TV shows that did *not* involve a purple dinosaur, she suddenly rolled over, looking very pensive.

"Daddy," she said very seriously, "I have something I need to tell you."

It wasn't lost on me at the time that those same words would most likely make me cringe ten years in the future. For now, however, knowing that she could not have stolen the car and was too young to be hooked on heroin, I played the part of the patient father and said, "What is it, Moon Pumpkin?"

"You know," she said, "I really don't like the letter H."

Well, I certainly wasn't prepared for that. I was well aware of the need to teach racial equality, but equality among consonants? And what about minority vowels? If I didn't nip this in the bud, the next thing I know she would start being mean to odd numbers (and don't even get me started on radicals). My head was spinning, and I had to get to the bottom of this or be damned to the Parental Hall of Shame for all eternity. But what to do?

I immediately thought of espousing the values of all twenty-six letters, but just as quickly dismissed it as being hypocritical. Sadly, I had a few reservations about the bipolar nature of the letter C myself, and to be quite honest had never been fully comfortable with Y's need to sometimes cross-dress as a vowel. Who was I to preach?

In the end, we compromised. She agreed to keep an open mind about all consonants and most vowels (she shared my distrust of Y), and I in turn would consider raising her allowance. We would treat all words as innocent, until proven otherwise, and would not dangle participles needlessly. Ultimately, the initially divisive experience brought us closer together. At least until she learned about hardcore G.

Rob Ballister

Rob Ballister is a retired naval officer and graduate of the United States Naval Academy. Upon commissioning, he attended flight school for about twenty minutes before finding out he had cancer. After Navy medicine patched him up, they told him he needed to find another job, and he was redesignated as a Civil Engineer Corps officer. As a CEC officer, he served in many construction and public works billets, and also with the legendary Seabees. Besides his operational Seabee battalion tour, the highlight of his career was serving as an instructor at the United States Naval Academy, where he taught engineering, naval weapons, and leadership.

Bit by the teaching bug, Rob knew that's where his future lay, and he currently is a Navy Junior ROTC instructor at a high school in south New Jersey. He works hard to teach his cadets leadership, citizenship, and self-discipline; occasionally, he teaches them new swear words by accident. A charter member of MWSA, Rob served as the lead reviewer for two years. He is the recipient of the organization's 2007 gold medal in the humor category for his first book, *God Does Have a Sense of Humor*, and the 2009 President's Award.

In addition to being a cancer survivor, Rob also success-fully battles depression in his spare time. He has spoken at numerous events in support of fighting cancer and prevent-ing suicide, and is a cancer mentor through the organization Imerman Angels. He lives in New Jersey with his wife Ivy, their two children Kyla and Grant, and their dog Hannibal the Wondermutt. He is working on his second book, but at the rate he is going, don't hold your breath.

Seabee Lieutenant Rob Ballister, "Wondering what I'm going to do about the huge concrete blocks we unearthed on our jobsite that weren't supposed to be there..." on the Rota Range Project.

27

A Demanding Mistress

Albert Ashforth

I continue to think about my decision to enlist in the Army at nineteen years of age even though it's over thirty years since I made it.

I'm doing okay, I guess. I live in a small city not far from Albany in upstate New York. I've got three rooms and a balcony, my government pension, a bank account, and in six years I'll be eligible for Social Security. I don't have a lot of friends, but I get together with some former military buddies from time to time, and that's enough.

I used to enjoy walking, but it's become more and more painful in the last couple of years. I'd like to be a little more active than I am, but all in all I can't complain. Some guys are way worse off. It's the prosthetic that bothers me most. I lost part of my left leg to an IED in Afghanistan nine years ago, and it's a nuisance just putting it on and taking it off. I sometimes think that if I hadn't decided to chase down those two characters that shot an RPG at our installation, I wouldn't have been running up a road in Khost when an IED went off. Of course, I never would have been in Afghanistan at all if I hadn't enlisted in the Army.

But there was another decision I made that I think even more about. My life today would be very different if, nine years ago, I'd listened to my girlfriend, Vanessa. From time to time I read about Vanessa and her husband in the *Wall Street Journal,* and they're even mentioned occasionally in the tabloid gossip columns. They live in a Park Avenue duplex and are high-profile contributors to the opera. Vanessa's father made news some years back when he sold his shoe firm to a wealthy sheik in the Middle East. Shortly afterward, Vanessa and her husband moved to New York City.

The Army promised to make a man out of me, and considering I was just a wet-behind-the-ears kid, they did a reasonably good job of it. Because I did well on the Army aptitude tests, my first assignment was with Military Intelligence in Fort Meade. In the course of my four years, mostly spent overseas in two MI detachments, I learned a good deal about the business of espionage—listening in, recruiting, and analyzing. I also learned how to maintain a low profile, to be skeptical of anything I was told by a person from another country, and to keep my mouth tightly closed. I even became mildly fluent in two foreign languages.

I liked the Army. I liked the military sense of order, the teamwork, and the opportunities I received to go places and do things I could never have done otherwise. And the Army liked me. My evaluations were uniformly good, and I guess that was the reason that, less than a year after my discharge, I received a call from a woman who asked if I would like to come to Washington and talk with some people.

When I got there, a bird colonel took me to dinner at a restaurant named Tabard, not far from DuPont Circle. He was a knowledgeable, funny guy, and just talking with him made me realize how much I missed the military. After dinner, we adjourned to the Army and Navy Club in Farragut Square, and toward the end of the evening, he asked me if I would be interested in a permanent job working for one of our nation's intelligence agencies. I said I would be.

After two decades of holding down a job as an intelligence officer on three continents, I decided to retire. But there is something they don't tell you when you sign on as a case officer: once you're in the espionage business, you can't ever really leave it. All that training has provided you with irreplaceable skills, and because you've probably acquired a fund of sensitive information, the government feels more comfortable when they can keep a close eye on you. There have been case officers who, after retiring, made a profitable sideline out of sharing what they knew with other governments' intelligence agencies.

So I guess it shouldn't have been a complete surprise that less than a year after retiring, I was again asked if I'd like to work for our government—but now on a contract basis. The World Trade Center attack had occurred without warning, and experienced officers were suddenly very much in demand. My first assignment took me to Africa, where I helped in chasing down some people who had blown up one of our embassies. For the next two years, I got offers on a fairly regular basis. The countries I visited included Macedonia, Germany, and Iraq.

It was during this time that I took my savings and, together with a partner, started a bakery business. We supplied rolls and pretzels to supermarkets and restaurants in a number of upstate counties, and the business made it possible for me to live the kind of life I'd always wanted to live. A comfortable one.

But by this time I had also acquired something else—an attractive girlfriend, a 33-year-old teacher named Vanessa. In the back of my mind I also had a thought that it was time, finally, to settle down.

But then Fred turned up. Fred and I had worked together in the Balkans. During a Friday evening dinner, we did a lot of reminiscing, and over dessert Fred suddenly asked me, "Would you like to go to Afghanistan?"

Fred's expression told me he and I suffered with the same affliction. He didn't say the words, but he could have. "Jerry, it's like being in love with a woman, hopelessly in love." I even remember how Fred watched for my reaction as he described the pay and benefits for signing on "just one last time."

I was undecided. Although talking with Fred triggered many memories, I told him I needed time to think things over. He said he'd need an answer by Sunday. What was really on my mind was the fact that I felt about Vanessa in a way that I'd never felt about any woman. But no matter how much I thought about it, I still couldn't make up my mind. It was an agonizing weekend.

On Sunday morning, I sat down at my kitchen table, a cup of coffee in front of me. Since Friday night I had thought of nothing but how Vanessa would likely take the news that I'd be leaving for Afghanistan for an unspecified period of time. Although I'd wanted to talk with her, I kept postponing the telephone call.

In addition to our personal relationship, I had something else to think about: a business opportunity that Vanessa's father was offering me. It would almost certainly make it possible for me to earn the kind of money it was impossible to earn in the bakery business. The offer was to become a business executive, and I'd continued to toy with the idea ever since Vanessa first mentioned it two weekends before.

As I sat in the kitchen, I recalled that conversation. Vanessa, who came from a small city in Franklin County and whose father owned a shoe factory in the area, said she couldn't imagine a nicer place for a wedding than her hometown church. When she mentioned that her parents were looking forward to her getting married, I said I didn't know she'd received a proposal.

"I'm only bringing up the topic, Jerry," Vanessa said, "because if I don't, who will?"

I asked who the lucky guy was, and Vanessa said, "I can visualize the two of us, me in my white dress and you in a dark suit. And all my girlfriends looking at you."

"Why?"

"They'll be jealous."

We'd spent a number of weekends talking like this.

I remember Vanessa rubbing her hands across my shoulders and saying, "You're not just good looking; you're strong."

"Sure, honey. I haul a lot of pretzels."

"There's something you should know, darling. Daddy says there will soon be an opening for a production manager, but he only wants to fill it with someone who's very responsible."

"Really."

"Jerry, I wanted to ask you...if you know anything about making shoes?"

"Only that they're made out of leather."

"But that doesn't mean you couldn't learn."

"About making shoes?"

"Yes."

"I'd rather be making something else."

"What?"

"Love. Wouldn't you?"

"Stop changing the subject. Daddy wants to meet you, Jerry. I've told him all about you. Listen to what I'm saying. There's going to be this opening in his firm. At first you'd be learning the business ..."

"I have my own business, honey."

"This is an opportunity, a once in a lifetime chance." Vanessa paused. "At least meet Daddy."

"I don't know if I'd be happy working in an office." I hesitated. "Maybe I would be. I don't know."

Vanessa was extremely attractive, but more importantly she had a wonderful personality and a great sense of humor. When we were together, I could feel the chemistry between us. It was tangible. I couldn't help thinking that I'd never again meet a woman like this.

Finally, I said, "I'm tied up this coming weekend, honey."

"How about the following weekend?" When I said that would be fine, Vanessa planted a damp kiss on my lips.

Just three days ago, hours before I'd talked with Fred, Vanessa had called. "Jerry, my parents want us to arrive at two o'clock, Sunday afternoon."

I said that was fine.

Vanessa's mother would be preparing a large meal. I'd be the guest of honor and the recipient of the family's unbridled hospitality. If I were now to tell Vanessa I had to cancel the visit and leave for an undetermined period of time, she would tell me she never wanted to see me again. And she would be correct in doing so. I won't even speculate on how her parents would react.

I could imagine her mother's tears.

There would be no way to explain this kind of decision.

I poured another cup of coffee—my fourth?—reached for the phone, but then thought better of it. Did I really want to go back overseas? Since I hadn't signed a contract, I knew it would still be possible to call Fred and let him know that my career as a soldier and intelligence officer was over—really over this time.

"Sorry, guys. Find someone else."

After a few more minutes, I'd made my decision. I poured a shot of brandy into my coffee, then another one. And only then did I pick up the telephone, look at it for a long moment, and begin to punch in Vanessa's number.

Albert Ashforth

After serving overseas with the U.S. Army, Albert Ashforth received a degree from Brooklyn College and subsequently worked on two New York City newspapers. Although he took his first newspaper job with the thought of becoming a cartoonist, Ashforth's first assignments were writing. On the basis of a newspaper article he wrote, he was offered a contract to write a book on the 19th century English scientist, Thomas Henry Huxley, a project that required two trips to London for research at the Imperial College.

Ashforth subsequently returned to Europe as a military contractor and has completed tours in Bosnia, Germany, Kosovo, Macedonia, and Afghanistan. He has worked as an instructor at Special Forces headquarters in Bad Tolz and trained officers at the German military academy in Neu Biberg.

Ashforth has written three books and numerous stories, articles, and reviews on a variety of subjects. His articles have been published in *American Scholar*, the *New York Times Magazine*, *Four Seasons*, the *Mystery Writers Annual* and other publications. Currently, he is working on a sequel to his novel *The Rendition*, which takes place against the background of Kosovo's struggle for independence. In the sequel, Alex is sent to Afghanistan to help solve the green-on-blue killing of a former Army buddy. *The Rendition*, which received the bronze medal from Military Writers Society of America in 2012, was recently a Kindle #1 selection in the Historical Thrillers category. *Publishers Weekly* described it as "an exciting spy thriller." Mr. Ashforth lives in New York City.

28

GIVING HOPE AND JOY

Lisa Remey

Grace Anne Remey, age eleven, may be one of Military Writers Society of America's youngest authors. She has been honored not only to share her books with other military and civilian kids but she is also involved in her local community. Since writing her first book at age eight, Grace Anne has actively volunteered. Her most recent community involvement has provided some unique opportunities both on base and in the local German community. Marissa Mordente, Spouse of 86th Airlift Wing Commander, describes Grace Anne's impact "between her books written and her volunteering in the military community and German community, as a rare treasure."

GenerationOn selected Grace Anne to be a Hasbro Joy Maker Ambassador in the fall of 2014. This honor meant she would receive 100 toys and then select organizations to "give joy" through local donations. Her first thought was to support military kids who had a deployed parent, but she also had a desire to give to local German children. With perseverance and the support from Ramstein base leadership and Ramstein Enlisted Spouses Association, Grace Anne was able to do both. Her first event consisted of teaming up with Ramstein Airmen and Family Readiness Center for a Disney *Frozen*-themed deployment dinner where over thirty toys were given to military kids who had a deployed parent. She enjoyed not only visiting with and passing out toys to other military kids, but also assisted at the face painting area. When reflecting on the event, Grace Ann remembers, "They all lined up and were anxiously waiting to get their toy that we wrapped. When it was one boy's turn, he ran over happily and right then he got the toy and opened it up, started building it, and now I see him walk around base with it." What an honor to support these families, as it takes courage for even the youngest child to deal with a deployed parent. Grace Anne shared, "It felt amazing taking all of the toys to the kids."

Next, Grace Anne was able to reach out to the German community which provided much joy for all. In order to make the donation, Grace Anne had key support from base leadership and the German Host Nation Office to plan, interpret, and locate the best local organizational fit for the donations. The Kinderheim St. Nikolaus, a residential group home, was selected and a meeting planned. It was a privilege to learn about and tour the local orphanage. Grace Anne learned about their mission of caring for children, teens, and young adults, and how they help families stay together. What an opportunity for a young military child to connect and give to local children. Marissa Mordente explains, "Grace Anne not only cares about other military children that are in her community but she also cares for those outside her community. This outreach improves our relationship with our host nation. She does this when reaching out to community children and brightening their day with toy donations and in doing so she is an ambassador who improves community relations."

Grace Anne was able to provide bundled gifts to seven residential groups of children as well as over thirty individual boys and girls who reside at the home.

After two community donations, Grace Anne never imagined there would be twenty-five games remaining. She selected USO Wounded Warrior Center as her third organization. The Center welcomed the donation of games, certain this would be an encouragement to transitioning troops and those receiving treatment at Landstuhl Medical Center. Landstuhl Medical Center serves as the nearest treatment center for wounded soldiers and sailors coming from Iraq and Afghanistan. Grace Anne met and handed out the remaining games to troops at a weekly dinner hosted in the center. Again, she was grateful for the opportunity.

You never know how sharing your story and becoming an author will reach others and touch your life in unexpected ways. It may be through giving support and encouragement to those who read your books, it maybe educating others about the military culture and your family traditions with people near and far, or it may be through unexpected opportunities to reach out and make a difference volunteering in your community. Mrs. Mordente explains how Grace Anne continues to help our whole community when she volunteers. "She impacts others to be like her, showing them they can do it, too, with the knowledge that you can make a difference in other people's lives," she said.

Lisa Remey

Lisa Remey is a Licensed Professional Counselor and Registered Play Therapist. Her counseling experiences range from using play therapy as a school counselor, private practice setting, and creating a program for disaster counseling in schools through FEMA, as well as time as a social worker. Lisa's primary role for the past twenty years has been as a military spouse, helping her family cope with seven deployments and many moves, as well as supporting military families through volunteer work.

Lisa has had the privilege to speak on topics regarding military families on the radio as well as at professional conferences in the United States and in Europe. In addition, she is a contributing author and publisher of *Lion's Pride: A Tail of Deployment* and *Lion's Pride on the Move.* Lisa is also the mother of Grace Anne Remey, author of the Lion's Pride books. *Lion's Pride: A Tail of Deployment* won a bronze medal in the children's book category from Military Writers Society of America.

Grace Anne is one of six youth honored as a 2013 Hasbro Community Action Hero Award by GenerationOn as well as a semi-finalist for Military Child of the Year. Grace Anne has a huge heart and enjoys sharing about military lifestyle with the community and helping other military youth and families cope with military-related stresses and challenges. Her pride of being a military kid shows through her love for art, writing, and sharing with others.

Grace Anne Remey, photo courtesy of Lisa Remey

29

THE HOPE
OF GOING HOME

Lila Sybesma

North of Memphis, Tennessee

April 27, 1865

Thunderous noise. Oppressive heat. It must have been about
three o'clock in the morning when I jolted awake. The deck
underneath me trembled and rolled, a second blast following
the first. The whole boat shuddered. Gabe woke up with a
start. "We're being fired on. Man your guns!"

"What happened?" I looked toward the bow of the boat.
The floor of the cabin deck was shattered in a thousand pieces;
much of the main cabin had simply disappeared. The social
hall, or what was left of it, filled with steam, the chandeliers
still glowing with an eerie light.

And in the middle of the boat, a cavernous hole.

The boat folded into itself. Wood splintering, the decks
above us collapsed like a house of cards. The wall lurched
to the right. Boiler fragments, bricks, and pipes blasted from
below. Timber cracked. Glass shattered. The wall ripped open.
Chunks of coal and charred wood flew through the air. A
plank speared past me and impaled a man, ripping through
his stomach and splintering through his back.

"We have to get out of here!" I tugged at Gabe. We trundled over limbs, legs, and feet.

"Come on!" Gabe pushed ahead.

He wedged in front of me, but I jerked him back. "We need to find Sarah!"

The cabin floor dropped down in front of me and made an inclined plane to the lower deck. Screams of soldiers echoed around me. Smoke rose out the chasm.

We tripped over soldiers on our way toward the ladies' cabins. I pushed back the curtain and barged through. A lady, matronly and round, her hair matted around her face, confronted us. "What do you want in here, sir?"

"Sarah. Where's Sarah?"

She peered over my shoulder, her eyes widening. "S-something's wrong with the boat." Her mouth gaping open, she backed away and pointed us toward Sarah's room. I shouldered open the door.

"Not here!" The berth was empty. No one was there.

The boat shuddered and a fire crackled where the boiler had been.

"There's a fire!" Gabe cried.

A dying choir of souls echoed, "Put out that fire, put out that fire!"

"Get a bucket!" We scrambled over the remains of the main salon to the railing and looked around. "I think they all blew off the boat," I yelled. Compared to screams around me, my voice was reedy and thin.

Then I saw it. The bucket Gabe had raised earlier was dangling on the railing, just out of my reach below me. I reached in my pocket for my jackknife, but of course it wasn't there.

If I only had my knife.

"We've got to get off!" Every time I grasped for the bucket, it flew from my fingertips.

O'Farrell! "We have to find O'Farrell! This way!" I tugged Gabe through the mass of men and debris. Men cried out as if shrieking from the grave. I stumbled over a beam lying diagonally across the deck. "Someone's pinned! It's O'Farrell. We've got to help him!"

We planted our feet on the deck, grasped the beam, and pulled.

"Pull!" I yelled. The beam wouldn't budge.

"Pull!" The beam lifted a few inches off the deck then sprang out of our hands. "We've got to try harder."

We both leveraged ourselves against the plank. "Pull!" The beam lifted a few inches. Gabe grabbed O'Farrell's arm and wrenched him from underneath the beam.

O'Farrell's knee gaped open, the white of his bone glistening through torn tissue.

I focused on his eyes. "You've got to swim."

After a glance at the water, O'Farrell turned toward me. "Can't swim. I'll drown."

"You won't." I gave O'Farrell a small board. "Hang on to this. You'll be all right."

O'Farrell clutched the board and examined it. While he stood rooted there another soldier ran up to him, grabbed the board, and dove off the boat.

Gabe wrenched off a door casing and shoved it in O'Farrell's face. "Here, tuck this under your chin."

"I can't swim a stitch. Will this casing work?" O'Farrell gave me a blank stare.

"Not if you're standing here," I said. "And once you're in the water, it won't be of any use unless you get away from the boat."

We helped O'Farrell to the railing. He turned to look at us with watery eyes. "Help me over."

I couldn't help him over. He didn't stand a chance. Gabe gave me a fierce look; then he helped O'Farrell over the railing. His legs and arms trundled through the air.

Gripping the railing, I stretched to find him. The water was a mass of men and horses. "O'Farrell!" I called. Then I saw him. His head bobbed above the surface yards away. I yelled as loud as I could. "Swim with all the mettle you've got!"

Chaos. Everyone on board grasped for life, the light of the fire flushed on their faces. Mutilated flesh peeled off their bones. The fire churned from the center of the boat, warping and braiding, in a twisted path to the sky. Twenty or thirty jumped off at a time. The river was black with men, their heads bobbing like corks.

O'Farrell flailed in the water, grasping and clutching. Gabe clutched the rail and peered into the water. "He's not going to make it. Not a chance."

Underneath me, soldiers thrashed in the churning water, reaching out for anything to keep them afloat.

"Throw barrels. Wood. Anything!" Gabe said. We both looked at each other.

"The alligator box!" I sprinted to the closet.

Someone had thought of the alligator box already. A soldier sliced his bayonet through the beast and dragged it out of the box by its tail. Slogging the box to the larboard side of the boat, he vaulted the crate overboard, and leaped after it. The water churned with men. Soldiers grabbed the bobbing crate, climbing over it, fighting for it. Men grasped each other, pulling others off of the prize.

Smoke stung my eyes. The fire's flaming tongue lapped at the edges of the boat; its burning fingers ran up my legs. I grasped the railing and peered into the flooded river, peppered with men. Leaving this boat without knowing where Sarah was tore something inside me. I was losing her all over again. If she was still on the boat, she needed me, but there was nothing I could do about it. Hemmed in by a wall of fire and the crush of soldiers, all I could do was jump, and hope she had, too. I looked back at Gabe, his face illuminated by the fire. Flames and smoke billowed behind him. I knew what we had to do.

I stepped to the edge of the boat. Only dozens of men bobbed in the water below me. I crawled on the railing and jumped off. Slamming into the water, I plummeted deep below the surface. My lungs starved for air. I clawed my way to the top and kicked off my shoes.

Gabe, a silhouette against the sky and the flames, stood completely still. Then he dove off. I waited an eternity for him to rise to the surface.

[Excerpted from *Yours*, the story of two brothers and their neighbor girl Sarah, all of whom were aboard the Sultana when its boilers exploded.]

Lila Sybesma

Dr. Lila Sybesma has written two books. *Memoir of a Man Between Wars* is a story about her father's service in WWII and Korea. *Yours*, a historical love story, is set in the Civil War.

Sybesma is a fourth-generation Iowa school teacher and a mother of three. When she's not writing, she's researching family history, managing weeds in her garden, or clocking miles on her motorcycle.

As a youth, Lila trekked through countless battlegrounds, forts, and battleships with her father. He would talk of her Scottish roots and border feuds. He shared stories of Revolutionary War, Civil War, and WW1 ancestors. He told of his own Korean War skirmishes. She learned one thing for sure—she came from a fighting family. But she never heard of the Sultana Disaster. When Lila rescued a book from family storage, she learned of her great-granduncle's plight. That little gray book was all it took: she was hooked on the *Sultana* story.

The *Sultana* was the worst maritime disaster in United States history. More lives were lost than on the Titanic; over 1,500 soldiers and civilians lost their lives. The boat, intended for 376 passengers, was loaded with almost 2,500 people, most of them soldiers. After surviving some of the Civil War's bloodiest battles—like Shiloh, Perryville, and Franklin—and after surviving prison war camps like Andersonville and Cahaba, they were finally going home.

Watercolor by Tom Cox, courtesy of Lila Sybesma

30

SHARING ALMONDS

Hudson Saffell

The morning was like all mornings in that season. The sun had risen fast and bright and was shedding fresh light on the valley.

But the sun would be no match for the darkness to come.

The new growth of the valley had turned green. For centuries, the soil there had been turned and turned by the calloused, sunbaked hands of the Hazara for centuries. The almond farming would have been good that year. The almonds would have been sweet and flavorful, sold and shipped throughout the country as they had been for ages.

No farmer knew the almond harvest would not last. Not until that early morning could the Hazara people conceive foreign shadows splitting the sunlight—Soviet helicopters swarming the sky over the fertile valley, the soil now bludgeoned with rockets. Whipping rotors and deafening eruptions alternately sounded—an invasive species of no natural cause.

MirAli was twenty-seven years old when the Soviet Army overtook his village in Daykundi Province, south central Afghanistan, 1979. He and several others ran from the fields to their homes to take up arms and protect their families, but were quickly overpowered, not only from above, but from below. Ground forces moved in. Within an hour of the attack, MirAli received shrapnel to his leg and, unable to flee, was captured.

I had the honor to meet MirAli in 2011. He was nearly sixty years old then and a sergeant in the Afghan National Army (ANA). He was one man of an entire company of ANA soldiers to arrive at our training camp in Southern Helmand Province, Afghanistan. MirAli immediately stood out among the rest, not because of his age, but because he held himself to a higher standard, and it showed. His military uniforms were always mysteriously pressed. His gear was always accounted for, packed methodically. His face, ever clean-shaven, exposed deep lines that mapped the proud, weathered face he held high, unafraid, true to the cause: a warrior's face.

It was on one of these days in 2011—I do not recall which—that MirAli was nicknamed "Chief," because he reminded us of the indigenous Native Americans we'd seen in history textbooks, novels, and films.

One of several qualifying mandates for an Afghan soldier to be inducted into our combat-training camp was the ability to read. Chief could neither read nor write, but we waived these rules for the sake of his military experience. We arranged literacy studies for him, which he took to most seriously and studiously, learning to read and write the alphabet and several phrases in his own language, Dari, and Pashtu as well.

No surprise to our team, Chief graduated the highly demanding combat courses we offered with honors, and instead of returning to his duty station—to his kandak—he accepted the highly revered position of permanent personnel instructor at our camp. He accepted without hesitation, standing shoulder to shoulder with us: an instructor among instructors.

In the evenings, some of the members of our weapons training team and a few interpreters and I would sit together with Chief on the stoop outside his tent, drinking chai and joking and laughing. His smile, though few teeth remained, was contagious and genuine. His voice always reminded me of Marlon Brando's method of speaking in *The Godfather*, but in Dari tongue.

I remember one particular evening, distinctly. It's one I will never forget. It had been a long day of training, and the season was turning. Chief, an interpreter, and I were gathered around, cracking almonds from their shells; I remember them being the very best almonds I've ever tasted. A quiet silence fell and then Chief began to narrate a story—his story. The cracking of almonds stopped as we listened to Chief. Behind his Brando voice, we could hear the remote-controlled spy planes taking off from miniature airstrips less than a mile away from our camp. We heard them like you can hear mosquitos near your ear, but did not listen to them. We listened to Chief.

"After my capture, the Russians tortured me," said Chief. "They broke my fingers and knocked out my teeth. God kept me alive because it was not my time. And I escaped...found my way to Pakistan. I returned one year later, found a small home with land and for a time, the farming was good. I was married and had a son."

Chief looked inside the chai kettle, then closed the lid and filled our little metal cups with a steady hand.

"But times became difficult as the Taliban regime took power. I lost my land and went to Iran to find a job. I worked there for a short while, sending money home, but when I returned several months later, my wife and son had been murdered during a civil war between villages. It was then I joined the Afghanistan Army. This is my country and these are my people. As long as I am alive, I will serve them."

We would never have drawn this kind of bead on Chief—that he was a man who had lived through so much anguish. How could an individual with such a gut-wrenching past be so forgiving, proud, and joyful? How did he live each day in gratitude for simply being alive and serving his country?

How is it that he was healthy, already surpassing the average lifespan of an Afghan male?

Perhaps strength is measured in many ways. There are those that encounter an obstacle and turn around in avoidance, never reaching their true destination. Others may experience an obstacle and fall apart—turn to dust. And then there are those like Chief, who appreciate life for what it is—the good, the bad, the unimaginable—every overcome obstacle strengthening the spirit.

It is 2015, now. I do not know if Chief is alive, but if he is, I know he is happy to be.

And I know that in the valley of Daykundi, the new growth is green, the soil fertile, the sun high and bright, and almonds harvested without fear.

Hudson Saffell

Hudson Saffell is originally from Ventura, California, and also lived in Chino Valley, Arizona, as a youth. He attended community college for two years in Ventura, where he read literary classics voraciously. He then began to write seriously, beyond the classroom. At age nineteen his cleverly titled vignette, "Vignette," was published in the literary journal *VC Voices*. The editorial panel told him the only reason he was published was because he "nailed Hemingway's talent for dialogue."

Hudson soon became restless on the west coast and moved to the east, living in Philadelphia for less than one year before again succumbing to wanderlust. He eagerly joined the military as a vehicle for travel and to gain more diverse experiences than those obtained sitting around at coffee shops writing about made-up stuff. Hudson went on to serve eight years active, enlisted duty in the U.S. Marine Corps, and loved the military life, earning the rank of sergeant in three years, spending a lot of his time overseas as a team leader in fifteen countries. He also spent a significant amount of time at sea. He served in Operation Iraqi Freedom and Operation Enduring Freedom, Afghanistan, respectively.

Recently, Hudson earned a bachelor's degree in American Studies from Penn State University and is pursuing a master's in English at Arcadia University in Glenside, Pennsylvania. His goal is to achieve the degree and teach writing in technical schools. Hudson's poetry was featured in the spring 2015 issue of *Bluestem* and a short story in *Exit 7*. He is also a freelance writer for GIJobs.com, a part-time library assistant, and a father to the most beautiful daughter you ever did see.

31

POEMS OF FAITH

Jon M. Nelson

Children Have Tomorrow

We must pass on our happiness and our sorrows,
To our children, for they own tomorrow.
The world is now theirs to take care,
We did our best but now we must share.
The children hold the key to the truth.
The world is now theirs, for they have youth.
The world we had was just to borrow,
We must save what we have to pass on tomorrow.
The children hold the future in the palms of their hands.
They must work together and united they'll stand
We must lead the children in the right direction,
By showing love and lots of affection.
The world belongs to the children we leave.
The future looks brighter, we all must believe.

I Stand Ready

I've fought for my country,
And shed my blood for you.
I help keep this nation free,
And defend the red, white, and blue.

I stand ready to defend,
On this and foreign soil.
My duty will have no end,
For my country I am loyal.

I stand to face my enemies,
If they decide to attack.
For you and your families,
I always have your back.

You can rest easy tonight,
Knowing that I am here.
I will stand ready to fight,
To help you calm your fear.

It is not always glorious,
There are times that I dread.
But I will stand victorious,
Until the moment I am dead.

Climbing

I have been down to the lowest level,
Where I stood face to face with the devil.
But I had to raise myself up higher,
And was able to get up out of the fire.

I had dug myself into a deep dark hole,
Where the emptiness would fill my soul.
I had found a way to raise my spirit,
To be able to get up out of that pit.

I have been to the bottom of the abyss,
Where I found that the world was amiss.
I had to climb up toward the light,
And I was able to escape that fight.

I've stood at the base of the mountain,
Where I knew I'd have to climb again.
But I would never be able to stop,
If I ever wanted to reach the top.

I have now reached the highest point,
And up here I hope I don't disappoint.
There's only one place left for me to go,
As I can see the stars beginning to show.

Leave Your Mark

When you're told you can't go on,
Or that you don't have what it takes.
Give it your all to prove them wrong,
And that they have made a mistake.

If someone makes you feel worthless,
And fills your head up full of doubt,
Give everything and nothing less,
Show them what you're all about.

We all have some kind of purpose here,
So show the world what you're worth.
Embrace your life without any fear,
While you're here upon this Earth.

You'll be heard if you raise your voice,
You can't start a fire without a spark.
It's your life so you must make a choice,
To always attempt to leave your mark.

Jon M. Nelson

Jon M. Nelson was born and raised in the great state of Minnesota in 1975. After graduating from high school in 1994, he worked a couple of different jobs for two years and realized he wanted something more out of life and wanted to see the world. He left for Basic Training at Fort Benning, Georgia, in the beginning of 1996 and has definitely seen much of the world since then. Jon is still actively serving in the U.S. Army as a sergeant first class, food service specialist, having changed his prior infantry military occupation specialty due to severe hearing loss.

Jon has earned the moniker of Soldier Poet by writing of his military experiences. As a combat veteran, he has seen the horrors of war firsthand and written tales about the battlefield. He has earned several awards for his poems, and his second of book of poetry, *Reflections of Life*, has earned a few book awards as well. He has just released his third book, *Brightness from the Shadows*, which focuses more on humanity and hopes to inspire mankind to be something better. Jon uses his writing to honor members of the military, veterans, and their families. His poetry touches on many subjects that can be read and shared by many audiences, even if they've never been a fan of poetry.

Jon hopes that his writing will in some way make an impact on the world, and make it a better place, even if it can change or inspire just one person. He is planning to retire from active military service very soon and is looking forward to pursuing his passion of writing for his full-time career.

32

FREEDOM FIGHTER

Farrell J. Chiles

Filipino Freedom Fighter to U.S. Army Officer

"My father told me us kids don't understand freedom, all the liberties we have and how we take things for granted," Ada Hurst said. "He passionately told me he would fight for this country again. He never spoke of how he suffered the torture, other than after a while of pain, the brain protects the body, and you feel no pain."

Background

April 9, 2015, marked the 73rd anniversary of the Bataan Death March. The Japanese attacked the Philippines on the same day they attacked Pearl Harbor, December 7, 1941. Three days later, the surprise attack was followed by a full invasion of the mainland of Luzon. By January 2, 1942, the Philippine capital of Manila fell to the Japanese. President Franklin Roosevelt sent a message on February 20, 1942 ordering General Douglas MacArthur to depart the Philippines. On March 11, 1942, General MacArthur left the Corregidor Island by PT boat, reaching the island of Mindanao, and from there flew to Melbourne, Australia. Japanese forces caused the surrender of American troops and Filipinos at Bataan on April 9, 1942. This surrender was the single largest one in the history of American military forces.

An estimated 63,000 Filipinos and 12,000 Americans were forced to march more than sixty miles from Mariveles, on the southern end of the Bataan Peninsula, to San Fernando, Pampanga. As many as 15,000 Filipinos and 750 American soldiers died during the march. Survivors were transported by rail from San Fernando to prison of war camps, where thousands more died from disease, mistreatment, and starvation. Many survived. Some escaped and renewed fighting until the Allied Forces were able to recoup and later win the war. One such survivor was Pablo E. Gonzales.

Pablo E. Gonzales

Pablo Gonzales was born on January 25, 1918, in Santa Ana, Philippine Islands, near the capitol of Manila. His parents were Cecilio and Ylumenada Gonzales. He had two siblings—a brother Celestino Gonzales and a sister Constancia. Growing up, Pablo only received a fourth grade education. He joined the U.S. Army at the age of nineteen as a private, on September 18, 1937. On June 5, 1939, he married Cristina Gialon. Their marriage produced five children. During the war, Pablo Gonzales served as a Filipino scout with Jose C. Calugas, Sr., who received the Medal of Honor for his actions during the Battle of Bataan. Gonzales and Calugas both later became American citizens and captains in the United States Army.

Early on January 6, 1942, Gonzales and his squad were assigned to reestablish severed communication lines. The Japanese heavy artillery positions were established. Heavy bombardment devastated U.S. and Filipino troops, causing survivors to scatter throughout the jungle. The last two surviving soldiers in Gonzales' squad were wounded and taken away. Gonzales remained alone and continued repairing the communication lines. Afterwards, he rejoined another group of soldiers actively engaging the Japanese.

On January 23, 1942, Gonzales received a special order that he was to receive a citation for a Silver Star due to his actions on January 6, 1942.

Later in the war, Gonzales led a guerilla group and obtained intelligence on Japanese movements and combat strengths, while conducting small-scale harassing attacks. Some of this information was relayed to officers who advised not to attack the Japanese. Believing the Japanese were massing forces at a certain location, Gonzales traveled a distance to personally meet with Lieutenant General A. Carlson, Battalion S-2, 20th Infantry, 6th Army, and Captain Chase of the 26th Calvary, Fort Stotsenburg. The information was re-evaluated resulting in a major successful assault against the Japanese.

The American troops were now in the Philippines in force and the Japanese were being defeated. On February 25, 1945, Gonzales received orders to report to San Fernando Pampanga 12th Replacement Battalion. On March 4, 1945, he officially became a member of the regular U.S. Army at the rank of staff sergeant, assigned to an artillery unit.

Gonzales continued to aggressively pursue the Japanese past the official surrender in September 1945. Organized attacks were still being conducted by Japanese troops unaware of the surrender. For his actions during combat, Gonzales received the Bronze Star Medal.

After the War

Gonzales, now a master sergeant, was commissioned a second lieutenant on August 22, 1947. On June 21, 1948, he was promoted to first lieutenant.

Gonzales again went into combat. He was deployed to Korea during the Korean Conflict and assigned to the 24th Artillery Division. He received his second Bronze Star for actions during combat. On February 24, 1953, Gonzales was promoted to captain and received orders for a three-year tour in Panama, stationed at Fort Davis. He was assigned to an artillery unit and assisted in the training at the jungle warfare and survival school at Fort Sherman, Panama.

Captain Gonzales retired from the military on May 30, 1959, after twenty-one years of military service. His awards and decorations include: the Silver Star Medal, Bronze Star Medal, Army Commendation Medal, Good Conduct Medal, Prisoner of War Medal, Army Defense Medal, American Campaign Medal, Asiatic-Pacific Campaign Medal, European-African-Middle Eastern Campaign Medal, World War II Victory Medal, Army Occupation Medal, National Defense Service Medal, Korean Service Medal, Philippine Defense Medal, Philippine Liberation Medal, Philippine Independence Medal, and the United Nations Medal.

After Military Service

Pablo Gonzales obtained employment working security jobs at the May Company and other department stores. These jobs were very frustrating after his successful career in the United States Army. He also found employment with Harbor General Hospital in Torrance, California, and with the Rancho Los Amigos National Rehabilitation Center in Downey, California, supervising a large staff of maintenance workers.

Family

Pablo and Cristina raised five children. The first two, Nor and Zer, were born in the Philippines. Oldest son Nor is an occupational therapist. Zer is a retired Los Angeles Police Department detective. Cecilia is a health care director. Ada is retired from AT&T and resides in Northern California. Paul is in Human Resources at DocMagic, Inc. in Torrance, California.

Ada further remembered, "When we lived in Lomita, California, we had a huge yard and my dad grew sugar cane. When we were small, Daddy would find a good sugar cane root, pull it up, and skin it with his machete (while gardening), and as a treat we would chew and suck the sweet nectar from the sugar cane."

Zer Gonzales recalls, "I learned discipline, integrity, and being a gentleman from my father." Displayed on the walls of his home in Southern California is his father's military shadow box exhibiting his awards and decorations. Also on the wall, in a case, are twelve bolos knives (similar to machetes) and Kris daggers from Pablo's days during World War II. He has a case displaying four samurai swords that his father confiscated from Japanese soldiers.

Cristina Gonzales died on October 7, 1980. Pablo Gonzales died of a stroke on February 28, 1993. They are buried together in Green Hills Cemetery in San Pedro, California.

Pablo Gonzales was a Bataan Death March survivor. He is a Filipino hero. He is an American hero. He demonstrated hope and courage. He left us with a proud legacy.

Farrell J. Chiles

Farrell J. Chiles is a retired United States Army Chief Warrant Officer and Vietnam Veteran with thirty-eight years of military experience. In 2007, he received the Distinguished Public Service Career Award from the Greater Los Angeles Federal Executive Board.

Farrell is the author of the book, *African American Warrant Officers: In Service to our Country.* The book tells the stories of unsung African American warrant officers who have served our country in and out of the military. This collection of historical articles, inspiring biographies, and profiles highlights the significant contributions of individual African American warrant officers from World War II to the present, with remarkable detail and language befitting their valor.

Chiles' first book, *As BIG As It Gets* chronicles the five consecutive years that he served as Chairman of the Board of the National Organization of Blacks In Government (BIG). He shares his thoughts on effective leadership, the power of networking, and his forward-thinking vision of BIG.

Farrell has written over two dozen articles on African Americans and others in the military, ranging from articles on World War II, the Korean Conflict, the Tuskegee Airmen, Buffalo Soldiers, and warrant officers. He has an extensive collection of books on African American military history. He is a collector and archivist and exhibits his collections of Frederick Douglass, Jackie Robinson, the Tuskegee Airmen, and the Buffalo Soldiers in libraries throughout Southern California.

He resides in Phillips Ranch, California.

33

CLOSE AS SHE GETS

Robert Goswitz

Quang Nam Province

Republic of South Vietnam

October 11, 1971

Red smoke curled over the log protecting the three GIs.

A bullet cracked the sky.

The sniper made Lieutenant Halvorsen jumpy. "Hey, Lansky, you got smoke? We need more cover."

Private Ed Lansky raised himself on his left elbow to remove a smoke canister from his web gear. He felt a sudden change of pressure near his right ear. A pulse of energy glanced off the crown of his steel pot, ripping it from his head. Lansky flattened himself behind the log, heart pounding, eyes wide open, staring at his helmet lying in the dust. The sniper round had torn the camouflage cloth cover and creased the metal underneath. A strange sonic *zing* lingered in the air.

"Keep your goddamned head down, Mister New Guy!" LT was angry. "Believe me, it's good advice!" His eyes closed, a patient pause. Opening his eyes, LT said, "You okay, Lansky?"

"Yeah, snapped my neck, but I can't feel any holes." His voice shook as he rubbed his scalp. "I'll keep my head down from now on."

"You're one lucky fuck, Lansky!" The anxious chatter from the other end of the log could only be Marty Allen's. "That would have been the end of most new guys."

Lansky attempted to sound confident. "I am lucky, always have been." He rolled onto his back, removed a smoke canister from his web gear, felt his hands tremble, took a breath, pulled the pin, and lobbed it over the log.

Yellow smoke.

Another bullet.

"That papa-san is a pain where a pill won't reach," said LT.

"A mongrel nipping at the heels of innocents." Lansky grinned at the lieutenant.

"Fucking profound, Lansky. Fucking pro-*found*." LT smiled sarcastically, surprised by the new guy's quick recovery.

"You musta read that somewhere, Lansky," Allen yelled. "You ain't that smart."

"Okay, okay. I read it."

"Gimme the phone, Lansky. Switch to air support."

Lansky changed the frequency on his field radio and gave his officer the radio handset.

"Time to give Pops something to think about while we make our getaway."

Lieutenant Halvorsen depressed the talk button. "Tomahawk Four-Niner, this is Lonely Boy Actual, over."

Lansky noticed sweat dripping off LT's chin.

"Tomahawk, this is Lonely Boy. Have sniper fire from the tree line at the top of the ridge. He's three hundred meters November Echo of my smoke, over."

A dust geyser erupted behind them.

"Roger-copy, Tomahawk, thanks, over and out." Looking at Lansky, LT said, "He's going to make his run now to cover our pickup bird."

A growling spot fell in the sea-blue sky. Gaining size and lethal shape, the gunship arced toward the ridge.

"So long, Pops," said LT.

Hidden hammers struck invisible anvils. The gunship opened with a long burst of cannon fire. Mushrooms of gray smoke and flying debris trampled the ridge. A fractured tree trunk bounced down the hill. White flame broke from the gunship. The mini-gun buzzed, evil, unnatural, the sound of five chain saws revved to full throttle. Wild dust clouds danced among the trees, suddenly stripping away leaves, branches, and bark. Flames exploded in the dry vegetation.

"Hey." The lieutenant nudged Lansky.

Behind them, helicopter vibrations grew suddenly intense. Flying below eye level, gaining cover in a sunken riverbed, the pickup bird closed on their smoke. Flashing above the riverbed, the Huey fanned sharply, sideways for a second, scrubbing off speed and then leveling into a delicate landing.

Ducking under the rotor blades, Lansky ran to the bird. He noticed a smile on the pilot's face. A bug-eyed caricature of the screaming eagle decorated his aviator's helmet.

They took off in a tight circle. Increased gravity pinned Lansky to the chopper floor. He caught a brief glimpse of the burning ridge. His dangling legs rose gently as they dived toward the water. The pilot leveled off twenty feet above the shallow river. The Huey accelerated. Emerald foliage on the bank blurred. The bird swayed side to side as the pilot negotiated each bend in the river.

A sampan blew into view. Three frightened river sailors hit the deck as the whirling machine shot overhead.

Looking back, Lansky saw a conical straw hat turning in the air. The wind caught his long legs pushing them back. Pulling them in, leaning against the bulkhead, he extended his large hands across the aluminum decking. His sodden uniform hung loosely on his semi-athletic frame.

Cool air rushing by dried him. He felt the exhilaration of being lifted out of a tight spot, smiling easy now, green eyes gleaming under his subtle brow.

Climbing, they flew straight across dry rolling hills dotted with villages and roads. A small, brightly painted green bus bounced along the dirt path below. Passengers sitting on the roof and hanging in the doorway looked up briefly as the Huey flew over.

The abandoned air base near Phu Bai came into view. Passing over the hangars, they settled down on a long concrete runway. Familiar fatigued dirty faces watched them step off. Lansky and Allen moved among the supine figures sprawled along the ribbon of concrete.

"Hey! Where ya been?" a grimy, sunburned soldier yelled at Lansky.

"Had to wait for an extra bird. Didn't get a ride on the first lift-out."

"Any trouble?"

Lansky lifted his steel pot up for all to see. "Had a sniper take a few shots at us. I think the Cobra got him."

A small group gathered to inspect the helmet, passing it man to man, fingering the creased metal and cracked inner liner.

Vernon Huddle shook his head. "That's about as close as she gets, Lansky."

[These are the first few pages of Goswitz's novel manuscript entitled *The Last Man in Vietnam*.]

Robert Goswitz

Robert Goswitz was born and raised in Chippewa Falls, Wisconsin, graduated from Milton College, and holds a master's degree in education from the University of Wisconsin Whitewater.

He was drafted into the U.S. Army in March of 1971 and served in Vietnam from September of 1971 to August of 1972 as a member of the 196th Brigade, the last American Army infantry unit in country. Goswitz was awarded the Combat Infantry Badge and the Bronze Star for his service.

After the military, Robert was a special education teacher from 1974 until his retirement in 2007. During his career he worked with cognitively disabled, emotionally disturbed, and at-risk youth in the Wauwatosa and Waukesha School Districts.

Robert lives on the banks of the beautiful Bark River in Hartland, Wisconsin, with Jody, his lovely, patient, and semi-saintly wife of thirty-six years. He is the proud father of two adult children. His son Robert is a supervisor for Whole Foods in Minneapolis, Minnesota. His daughter Andrea is a high school art teacher in Fort Atkinson, Wisconsin. One of his short stories, "Setting the Woods on Fire," will be published in *O Dark Thirty Literary Magazine* this year. He is currently seeking representation for his first novel, *The Last Man in Vietnam*.

34

BATTLE OF THE CORAL SEA

Phil Keith

This excerpt is a fragment from the frantic action of May 8, 1942, the last day of the Battle of the Coral Sea. The doomed USS *Lexington*, CV-2, is under furious attack by nearly 100 planes from the Imperial Japanese Navy aircraft carriers *Shokaku* and *Zuikaku*:

**1115: "Agnes Red," 12,000 feet,
Ensign Edward R. "Doc" Sellstrom**

The young aviation cadet from Iowa wanted to be a doctor but the war had disrupted his plans. He signed up for pilot training and by March 1941, he had been commissioned an ensign and had his wings. In the February clash when Butch O'Hare earned his Medal of Honor, Sellstrom was awarded a Navy Cross for downing a Japanese flying boat as well as one of the Betty bombers that was trying to sink *Lexington*. His skill at gunnery and his terrific flying had earned him a spot as his skipper's wingman. That's exactly where he was shortly after 1100 on May 8, on LCDR Ramsey's wing as he, Ramsey, and ENS George Markham (designated cohort "Agnes Three") struggled to get high enough to intercept the Japanese bombers bearing down en masse for the Lady Lex.

Finally, at 1109, Sellstrom spotted them. "Skipper! Eleven o'clock right up from you. Can't you see them straight up from you?" he shouted into his radio.

Ramsey saw them, but he didn't know what he was looking at. Were they bombers or fighters or both? He became fixated on getting higher, getting in among them, whatever they were, and shooting down as many as he could.

Sellstrom glanced over his shoulder and caught sight of something even more chilling than the mass of enemy aircraft above: Shimazaki's torpedo bombers were zooming in from below. He could see no other defenders anywhere nearby.

"Skipper!" he shouted again, "Look down! Torpedo bombers, headed for the task force!"

Ramsey did not reply, still focused on the planes above. Sellstrom had a split second to make a decision. He could continue to struggle for altitude, to get behind the threat above, then try to chase it down; or, he could dive immediately on the targets below, guns blazing.

Without permission, he peeled away and plunged downward. Sellstrom knew he was risking the wrath of his commanding officer but he believed the torpedo planes were the greater threat.

Sellstrom was on the torpedo bombers before they knew he was there. With the advantage of the tremendous speed he had picked up in his dive, he sliced through the right-hand side of the rearward "vee" and cleanly picked off one of the Kates, which flamed up and spun into the water. This got the immediate attention of three of the Zeros. Rolling, spinning, and diving, the four planes careened after one another through the clouds.

1116: Japanese Torpedo Strike, Initial Attack, LT Shimazaki

Shimazaki's torpedo attack juggernaut rolled on. A minute later, four miles out from *Lexington*'s, the thirteen remaining Kates blew by and through the screen put up by eight Dauntlesses from *Yorktown*'s VS-5. The scouts were caught between Shimazaki's "vees" with no time or altitude advantage. Several of the hapless pilots never even witnessed the torpedo planes speeding by, but a moment later they felt the sting of the Zeros. In rapid order, LTJG Earl Johnson, ENS Samuel Underhill, and ENS Edward B. Kinzer were blasted from the skies, their Dauntlesses flaming and spinning into the sea. ENS Kendall Campbell's SBD had its tail blown off by a buzz saw of cannon fire before looping crazily into the waves. Kinzer had dropped a 1,000-pound bomb on *Shoho* the day before, Johnson had earned a Navy Cross for heroism in the attacks on Tulagi, Underhill, a graduate of Yale and Harvard Law School, had also bombed *Shoho*, and Campbell had earned a Navy Cross for the New Guinea raids. Four brave pilots, all holders of the Navy Cross, dead in under a minute. Each would have a destroyer built and named after him in the coming months.

It was beginning to look as if Captain Sherman's pet theory concerning the Dauntless as a faux fighter was being blasted full of holes, but the *Lexington*'s screen of SBDs would have better luck. Scouting Two had taken a higher altitude than VS-5 and by the time Shimazaki's planes were nearby they had started to descend even lower, easing back their speed to drop their weapons. Nine SBDs swung around and chased the Kates, who were, by then, only 5,000 yards from their drop points. VS-2 did not have to face the Zeros, either, at least at first: the Japanese fighters were tangling with the remnants of VS-5 and three of them were still trying to shoot down Sellstrom. Before their escorts returned to cover them, Shimazaki lost two Kates to the pilots of VS-2.

***

One of those two doomed Kates was shot down by LTJG William E. Hall, a scout pilot from VS-2. Hall had already tasted victory on May 7 when he had been one of the pilots to drop a 1,000-pound bomb on the unfortunate *Shoho*. Later on that day, May 8, after the torpedo and bomb attacks against *Lexington* and *Yorktown* had been completed, and the Japanese began to run for home, a grand melee developed between the fleeing planes and the American pilots defending their ships. The Japanese Zeros became particularly aggressive. Two Zeros jumped LTJG Hall and riddled his plane with bullets. Hall was seriously wounded in both ankles from fragments coming up through the bottom of his ship, but he somehow pushed through the pain and executed a series of deft maneuvers to escape the Zeros. Hall and another VS-2 pilot, ENS John Leppla, went after the four antagonizing Zeros with a vengeance and between the two of them shot down three of the Zeros. Fighting blood loss, pain, and immobility in his lower legs, Hall somehow managed to get his plane back to the *Lexington* where he executed a near perfect landing despite his injuries and the severe damage to his Dauntless. Medics hauled the nearly comatose Hall out of his aircraft. The plane captains took one look at Hall's riddled ship and simply decided to push it over the side. Hall's heroics over two days of intense combat earned him one of the four Medals of Honor to be earned at the Battle of the Coral Sea.

Phil Keith

Phil Keith holds a degree in history from Harvard and has done master's work at Long Island University and the Naval War College. After graduating from Harvard, Phil went directly into the Navy and became an aviator. During three tours in Vietnam, he served with distinction and was awarded, among other decorations, the Air Medal, the Presidential Unit Citation, and the Navy Commendation Medal.

After his wartime service, Phil rose to the rank of captain in the Navy Reserve and is also a licensed U.S. Coast Guard captain and master's mate. As a business executive, he worked for two Fortune 500 firms and is a former assistant professor of business at Long Island University. Since 2007 Phil has been an adjunct instructor at the Rhode Island School of Design, teaching marketing and writing courses.

To date, Phil has authored two novels and three nonfiction books. His Vietnam book, *Blackhorse Riders*, won the 2012 award from USA Book News for Best Military Non-Fiction, was a finalist for the 2013 Colby Award, and earned a 2013 silver medal from Military Writers Society of America. His second Vietnam book, *Fire Base Illingworth*, was released in 2013. His latest book is *Stay the Rising Sun*, an account of the crucial World War II Battle of the Coral Sea and the loss of USS *Lexington*, CV-2, in May, 1942. Phil is currently writing *America and the Great War*, a 100th anniversary commemorative on America's involvement in World War I.

Phil serves on the planning board for the Town of Southampton, New York, and is a life member of VFW Post 5350, American Legion Post 924, the Disabled American Veterans, and Vietnam Veterans of America. He lives in Southampton with his partner Laura Lyons and son Pierce.

35

TOP

Richard Geschke

Damn, there I was in my quarter-ton jeep, stuck in an infernal mud hole in Grafenwoehr Germany looking at my driver who said the mud hole posed no problem. As I stepped out onto the muddy pine barrens of Graf, another jeep was approaching with a ramrod-straight first sergeant riding shotgun. I recognized him immediately as our company's First Sergeant Schmidt, a combat veteran of three wars.

Looking at my predicament as the executive officer of A Company 1st Battalion 7th Infantry he immediately called for another jeep for me and proceeded to dress down the bewildered driver for not properly utilizing government property. This was one of many instances that "Top" (military slang for first sergeant) saved my young butt from potential disaster. He was an old-school military lifer who although he was enlisted, was known to take care of junior officers whom he favored.

He struck an imposing figure with his short gray cropped hair sitting on his head and covering a face well creased as a solid veteran Army lifer. He was about six foot two inches in height and in guessing his weight I would say he was 220 pounds. To guess his age at this time (1970), I would put him at forty. All junior officers in the company, to include the commanding officer who was a captain, treated him with respect and admiration. Among his decorations were a Bronze

Star with V device and a Purple Heart Medal, along with Combat Infantryman's Badge with a star. This meant he fought as an infantryman both in Korea and Vietnam.

Nobody argued with Top, as he was respected by both the senior NCOs and the officer cadre. To add additional mystique to the legend the story goes as follows:

First Sergeant Schmidt was not really German; in reality he was of Polish descent with a last name of Senovich. Living in Poland during World War II, young Mr. Senovich lost his family to include his father and all his siblings to the invading Russians in 1944. The only surviving member of his family was his mother. With the Russians bearing down on the out-numbered Germans, young Mr. Senovich changed his surname to Schmidt and joined the German Army to fight the Russians on the Eastern Front.

Once the war ended, he and his mother were among the many displaced people wandering the ruins of a defeated Germany. They ended up in a displaced person camp in West Germany where eventually they got passage to the United States in or around 1948. He and his mother ended up in Detroit, Michigan, where Mr. Schmidt found employment at a General Motors assembly plant and sought the American Dream.

In June of 1950, the sounds of guns emanated from the battlefields of Korea and draft conscription accelerated to feed the hungry military to fight the evil forces of Communism cloaked in the auspices of North Korea and Communist China. Private Schmidt arrived in 1951 and saw combat action at The Battle of Old Baldy as an infantryman in a machine-gun company. As a draftee, young Private Schmidt was promoted to corporal, and upon reenlistment, he was a buck sergeant. So by 1953 Sergeant Schmidt decided to become a career soldier.

Here was a Wehrmacht soldier who fought for the Third Reich committing himself to the service of the United States of America. True to his word, when the time came he served in Vietnam. His tour of duty was with the 101st Airborne Division where he fought in one of the most reported actions of the war, Hamburger Hill. His descriptions of this action showed junior officers committing tactical mistakes and fatal errors of inaction. Later as a first sergeant he conveyed to the junior officers he favored (myself among them) what mistakes they had made and how to avoid them on the fields of combat.

Fast forward to 1970 when I first walked into A Company 1st of the 7th Infantry's orderly room in Aschaffenburg, Germany, where I found a gray-haired first sergeant saluting me and asking what I wanted. From that time forward, Top guided me as to what I should do and how I should do it. I found out soon enough as an executive officer how to conduct myself in maneuvers in Grafenwoehr, Germany, and later in training exercises in Vilseck.

In November 1970, a week before Thanksgiving, the 3rd Brigade of the Third Infantry Division conducted field maneuvers in Granfenwoehr for an entire week. During maneuvers our infantry track vehicles darted forward and backward, going from point to point in the pine barrens of Southern Bavaria. The need for expertise in navigating vehicles from point to point in nasty pre-winter weather was a demanding reality. Being an infantry leader demanded that the vehicles negotiate the terrain where they engaged targets of opportunity and also points of enemy strength.

Maneuvers of going back and forth may sound simple. Simple it was not, and the junior officers and senior enlisted men are paramount in the negotiation of getting one's unit to the correct coordinates. During these maneuvers in Graf, I found that my company commander was well schooled in map reading. And as good as he was, I found out on the internal radio communications that First Sergeant Schmidt was even better in both terrain analysis and map reading. In fact, throughout the maneuvers Schmidt was able to locate our position within five meters.

I was given a night assignment in Graf to advance in the pitch blackness to the battalion command post with a prisoner and a coded message for the battalion commander Gregory P. Dillon. Given the coordinates by my company commander, I proceeded to the location and found only track evidence of occupation, but in fact no command post. I went back to my jeep to report by radio communication that no one was present. As I sat down in the jeep, I felt a crunch as I severed the communication wire from my microphone to the radio. Here I was with no communications and no way of conveying my situation.

When I finally reported to my company commander, I was dressed down and accused of failing my mission. I did fail to find the command post. The fact remains that I did locate the coordinates given to me. What was missing is that my company commander gave me old coordinates and did not give me the updated coordinates as transmitted to him. He was in error.

Top knew of this error and told me as much. I was not to blame and Top proved it. He had the courage to tell the truth, and for that I see him as an honorable man who told it as it was. It mattered not what uniform he wore, as he lived the code of a true warrior.

Richard Geschke

Richard Geschke was born and raised in Cleveland, Ohio, during the late 1940s, 1950s, and 1960s where he attended a Catholic parochial school and John Marshall High School, graduating in 1965. He graduated from Kent State University in 1969 with a degree in comprehensive social studies from the College of Education and an Army ROTC commission. He served from 1969 to 1972 in the infantry in Germany, Panama, and Vietnam. Upon completion of his army service, Geschke met his future wife Ann and started a family in the late 1970s with the birth of a daughter and son. Mr. Geschke has been employed in the automotive industry to the present time.

Geschke has been published with letters to the editor in the *New York Times*, the *Washington Post*, the *Chicago Tribune*, the *Christian Science Monitor*, and the *Hartford Courant*. He has also been published with op-ed pieces in the *Bristol Observer*.

With longtime Army buddy Robert A. Toto, Richard co-authored their Army memoirs titled *In Our Duffel Bags: Surviving the Vietnam Era*. Their book was awarded a 2012 silver medal in the memoir category by Military Writers Society of America. The duo followed up their award-winning memoir with a book of poetry titled *Shadows of Combat: Poetry about the Vietnam Era*.

Richard is an active member of Military Writers Society of America as a book reviewer and member of the judging committee. He currently resides with his wife in Bristol, Connecticut, and enjoys visits from the children and grandchildren.

36

IEDs

Caroline LeBlanc

Nina looked through the mail on the kitchen table. A brochure's banner waved like a flag: Life's Too Short to Clean Your Own Home.

Damn right! Nina thought. Except now she cleaned other peoples' houses to pay her bills. It wasn't always like this. Before Iraq, she made decent money as a home health aide. In Iraq, the Army paid her tax-free dollars to drive vehicles through IED country. But then, cleaning houses was a lot easier than searching desert women in burkas or scraping body parts into body bags.

The clock read 6:30, and Dave wasn't home from work with the baby. Soggy hamburger helper simmered on the stove. All hell must have broken loose in the emergency room. Dave always called if he was going to be late. Nina grabbed an apple to tide her over.

How had things ended like this? After high school, she'd worked full time and made decent progress toward her nursing degree. Her reserve hitch gave her a few extra dollars and GI Bill tuition money. Now, the thought of broken bodies paralyzed her.

After 9/11, she had hoped she could graduate before her unit deployed. Then, Dave filled the staff nurse slot in the unit. First chink in her plan: pregnancy. Second: marriage. When her unit finally deployed, she stayed behind to deliver

Ben. A short maternity leave, and she was off to Iraq. Ben stayed with his grandparents.

Grandma Betty had him Monday to Friday, and Nina's mom Rita took him on weekends. While Nina ate sand and dodged IEDs, Betty and Rita raised Ben for nearly the first year of his life. Now, he was going on two years old. Between Nina's hours at work and school, Betty still spent more time with Ben than Nina did.

The phone interrupted her thoughts.

"I'm at Mom's," Dave blurted. "Dad has chest pain, but refuses to go to the hospital."

"Is Ben okay?"

"Ben's fine, just cranky."

"Why not call 9-1-1?"

"No use. They can't force Neil to go."

"Times like this, having just one car sucks."

"Could your mom come get Ben? I need to hang here."

"Rita doesn't drive after six o'clock."

"Couldn't she make an exception?"

"Not a good idea, Dave."

"Just this once, Nina?" Dave huffed.

When Nina called, Rita had already downed a few Budweisers. She wasn't happy about missing her programs, but she said she'd be over in thirty minutes. It took her an hour.

Nina got in the car and drove to Neil's.

The TV's blare cut through the locked door. Nina pounded for what seemed like ten minutes before Dave opened it.

"Rita's sleeping it off in the car, and I have class early tomorrow," she shot.

"Sure. Ben's with Dad. Go in while I get Ben's stuff?"

Nina sighed. "How's Neil?"

"Oriented to date, time, place, and complaint of the day."

She stretched a smile on her face.

"Hey, Neil. Rough day, huh? I'm here for Ben."

Neil grunted. His eyes never left the screen. Ben curled under his blanket on the couch. Nina breathed him in, warmed into her first real smile since leaving him and Dave that morning.

Neil's gagging cut through the TV cacophony. Sweat rolled down his face, copy-paper white. He crumpled to the floor. Nina screamed for Dave. She checked Neil's pulse—thready. Breath shallow, then gone. As she started CPR, her eyes glazed.

Tanya had slept in the cot next to Nina. Both were medically cleared after the IED had torn up their convoy two days before. In the 2 a.m. dark and cold Tanya began thrashing, arms and legs banging the tent wall and her bunk until everything stopped: the thrashing, the breathing, the pulse Nina felt for. She thumped on Tanya's heart. "Beat, damn you. Beat." As the docs carried Tanya away, Nina looked at the bedside picture of Tanya's three-year-old daughter. Tanya didn't even make it to Medivac.

"Nina! Let me take over!" Dave roared.

"I got it! Just breathe for him!" Nina shouted.

"Switch!"

"No! Did someone call 9-1-1?"

"Mom did. Switch!"

"In a minute. Get some air into him. Who's screaming?"

"Mom—at the 9-1-1 operator."

Dave put his mouth over Neil's.

***

The EMTs shut off the TV. While they took over, Nina gave a full report. They stabilized Neil, and rushed him to the ER Dave had left a few hours earlier. He trusted these guys. They brought him this kind of thing every day, but he decided to sit this one out. Ben slept through it all. Nina bundled him up.

She and Dave locked eyes. Like the old days. Teamwork—and that adrenaline ride.

***

At the hospital, Dave pondered calling his sisters. He flashed to his seventh birthday, the day his seventeen-year-old twin sisters had disappeared. The day he lost three mothers. Nobody said anything. When he got home, his sisters were just gone, and his mom was staring at the wall.

In the cardiac bay, a treatment team worked on his dad. Dave settled Betty in front of the waiting room television so he could have a cigarette in the parking lot while he called Nina.

"Dave?"

"How'd you know it was me?"

"Who else wakes me at this hour? Reminds me of when you went off to the sand box and left me behind, fat and pregnant."

"Those were o-dark-thirty calls, weren't they?"

"They were," she purred.

Dave's tone changed. "You were somewhere else when you were pumping on Neil."

"Forgot where I was for a minute."

"A minute!"

"Not the time, Dave. How's Neil?"

"No change. Mom's spaced in front of the waiting room TV. I came out for a breather." Dave sucked on his cigarette. "Need to get up the courage to call my sisters."

Nina's breath caught. "Maybe you should wait until something is more certain."

"You think?" Dave hoped he didn't sound too relieved. "Did you get Ben down?"

"Grandma Rita did. She's asleep on the couch. I convinced her I'll need her help in the morning."

"Did you know Rita had valium? We have her—it—to thank for calming Betty down." He took another drag. "Look, Nina. Betty won't be able to babysit tomorrow..."

"Everything's under control. Ben can go to campus day care."

"Day care? Don't you need to register him, provide proof of immunization and shit?"

"Done. I've been waiting for the right time to tell you."

"But..."

"Time's right, Dave. Betty and Neil need you. But you'd better call me with progress reports," she teased.

"Are you sure about this, Nina?"

"Sure as I am about anything."

"What will Betty do without Ben?"

"We'll see. She has her hands full for the foreseeable future."

"It will crush her."

"I want my baby back, Dave. Ben starts day care tomorrow."

Dave felt far away. "Can we afford it?"

"We'll make it work."

"I don't know."

"Life's too damn short, Dave. Go check on your parents. And don't hurry to pull your sisters into the mix." Then, tenderly, "I love you, Dave."

"Okay. I'll call you when I know more." Nina waited out the silence until Dave said, "I love you, Nina."

He tapped "End" as he walked toward the hospital.

Caroline LeBlanc

Caroline LeBlanc, former Army nurse and civilian nurse psychotherapist, has had her poetry and essays published in the United States and abroad. In 2010, Oiseau Press published *Smokey Ink and a Touch of Honeysuckle*, her chapbook about life as an Army wife, and the descendant of 17th Century Acadian/French Canadian settlers in North America. She regularly contributes interviews and book reviews to *Poetry Matters*, a blog staffed by Spalding University alumni.

As Writer in Residence at the American Military Family Museum, Caroline wrote the script for the museum's traveling museum exhibit; co-produced and created the script for Telling Albuquerque and *4 Voices* stage performances; facilitated *Standing Down*, a New Mexico Humanities Council book discussion group for veterans and family members; and hosted the Women Veterans Writing Salon in Albuquerque.

Before leaving the Fort Drum, New York, area in 2012, Caroline offered Writing For Your Life programs to wounded warriors and military family members. In 2011, Spalding University awarded her a master's degree in creative writing. Her visual art has been in numerous group shows in New York and New Mexico. She is a founding member of the Albuquerque based Apronistas Collective of women artists who regularly mount community art shows highlighting women's rights and ecological issues. Since 1969, she has been an Army wife, and she has been an Army mother since 1995.

Photo courtesy of Georgia Garrison Training Center,
Fort Stewart, Georgia

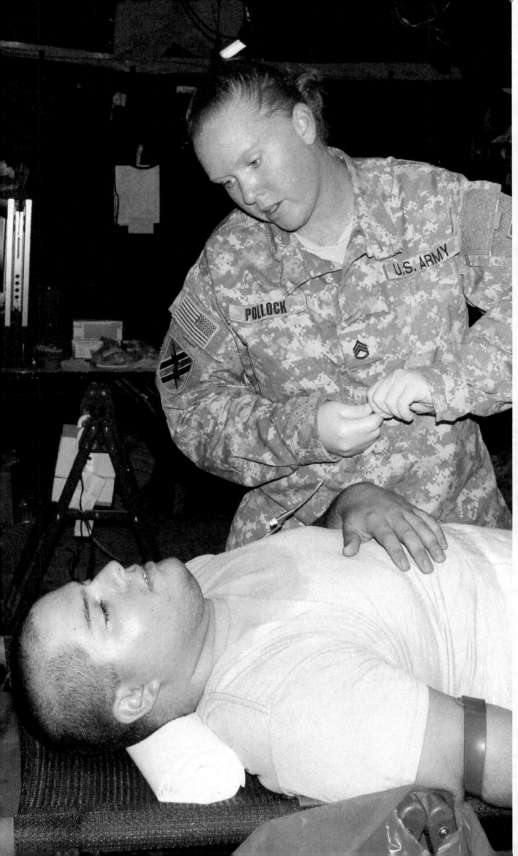

37

MAKING THE TURN AT THIRD

Robert M. Pacholik

"Look. I don't think this is...going to..." Brownie said, shifting his weight from his left foot to his right foot, like a boxer expecting to take a heavy body blow.

Dana looked at him knowing that if he kept talking, she would burst into tears. She was not going to cause a scene and cry, dammit. She would not.

Brownie couldn't help himself. He was getting on a plane for Algiers. God knows why. He was leaving her, but he couldn't explain why he was doing it, not even to himself. It was late May 1954, at Midway Airport on Chicago's South Side, Gate 8.

The four-engine Super G Constellation had already fired up one of the starboard-side engines, and he knew he needed to go. Midway Airport was not crowded, but it seemed absolutely desolate at that moment.

"You better...it's ..." she sputtered knowing how klutzy and dumb it all sounded. She was an ace reporter for the *Chicago Tribune*, and hell, she could talk her way into the Nuremberg War Trials and come out with a pre-suicide interview with Hermann Goerring.

Tough. Good looking. Capable. But not, when it came to men. She always went after the "bad boys."

They had met in London nearly a year ago. She was covering something, and she attracted him like a lightning bug on a summer night. Two days together in a swanky hotel room and he was in trouble all over again.

Brownie did something on oil well rigs, but he didn't move or smell like a roustabout. He was six foot one, with brown hair and the sea-green eyes of a housecat. He wore shirts with collars and contrasting slacks that showed he knew how to dress. He could carry on an interesting conversation, knew about books, and had some sort of family breeding that said he would be a good catch.

So why was he gonna go there? He couldn't explain it to her because he couldn't even unsnarl it for himself. He liked her. He wanted her. All that fondling, nuzzling, and undressing, and here he was leaving her and going to drill holes in the sand 13,846 miles away. The French had just lost whatever the hell it was they were fighting for, and now some sheik he'd met at Southern Illinois University, Carbondale, invited him to come and drill holes in the desert. Stupid idea if there ever was one. They offered him scads of money for his time, but would that make any difference after five or six months on a drilling rig with pipe, mud, and dirty, ugly men?

She honked into the small lace handkerchief she clutched in her right hand, her only real concession to the female agenda. Should she just spill her guts and tell him how much she loved him?

Brownie was dawdling near the last velvet rope stanchion that separated the first-class passengers from the riff-raff that flew cattle class.

"I-I really have to..." Brownie said, and then he turned and started down the stairs that led to the tarmac.

"Couldn't you just take the next flight?" she said with that last gasp of hope in her voice.

He stopped midstride and nearly got run over by the businessmen, secretaries, steel executives, and financiers.

"Well, now what the hell do I do?" Brownie said, muttering to the underside of his Brooks Brothers fedora, looking desperately at the empty spaces between people.

The stewardess saw that he had stopped in the middle of the pack and was obstructing the flow down the stairs and across the tarmac to the boarding ramp.

"Sir, do you need some help? We have a schedule to keep, and we'd really appreciate it if you kept moving toward the aircraft," she said, looking all trim and curvy and perfumed all fresh-strawberry luscious.

She wasn't exactly there to usher him into the B-17G nine years before when the 43rd Bomb Group made their second and then third terrible series of raids on Schweinfurt and later Dresden. He could still picture it.

Crawl in through the upside-down entry port with your ass hanging in the air, shinny down the narrow catwalk over the bomb bay, and settle in next to the .50-caliber waist gun that was your miserable job.

Rinney, the left-side waist gunner got killed outright on the last mission. Taslowski nearly bled to death before his blood froze and stopped the hemorrhaging in the tail turret. The ME-109s swept in so close you could barely acquire the target, but he fired wildly anyway. LaSuto, the top-turret gunner/radio operator just kept screaming even after the two Nazi planes came head-on and strafed the left-side pilot's windshield. Lieutenant Gorman, the co-pilot, just flew on in total silence in the ripped-up, howling drafty cockpit. Thank God, Miller calmed us all down after we had dropped our bombs and were headed home.

Ambrose, the bombardier, navigated us down to 1,450 feet after the fighters broke up the formation and started picking off stragglers. We "hunked and chunked" our way through the cloud cover, flying higher, then lower, then higher than before, swerving left and right in crazy angles, just to confuse the ack-ack guns.

Welcome aboard.

Brownie was still stopped, and Dana's emotions were still boring a hole in the back of his head while he stood there on the concourse.

"Couldn't I just bring her aboard as luggage and get married in Tangiers?" Brownie said, half-whispering to himself, before some clod from International Harvester bumped into him and told him to keep moving.

"I guess not. She wouldn't exactly like it there because it's so damn hot. Overhead fans can only do so much, and most nights are just a sweat bath of soiled linens," he muttered, and then he realized he was walking back to the terminal gate.

Dana was sobbing and sniffling, and happy, and glowing like a morning glory when he walked back over to her.

"Can we just go get a cup of coffee and a doughnut or something? I don't like flying on an empty stomach," Brownie said, not really looking at her face. Brownie took her arm, and the sleeve of her white linen pantsuit, and steered her toward some sort of sit-down café in the main terminal.

The waitress was a gum-chewing Mildred who took his order for two coffees and two frosted cake donuts, *tout suite.*

"Dana, I'm not young anymore. I'm pretty well set in my ways. I just don't know how..." he blathered on.

She honked into her linen handkerchief again, which was by now a crumpled wet rag in her right hand. She dabbed at the edges of her bloodshot eyes. She was absolutely carnally radiant at that moment.

"Does the Trib have a bureau in Egypt or Tunis? Maybe we could bushwhack back and forth for a while and stay together by teletype. How's that sound?" Brownie said.

Now she was just staring at him, characteristic for a statuesque, brunette international "tough-guy" gal reporter who would go anywhere and always got her story.

"Dana? How does that sound? Say something, Dana," he said, squirming in the fake red leatherette booth overlooking the taxiway and the main runway.

Mildred brought two coffees, two dark-brown overcooked doughnuts and asked, "Anybody take cream?"

"What? No. No, we're fine."

"Will that be all today?"

"Yes, we're fine."

Mildred slapped the green striped receipt down on the table between them. *Let them figure out who would pay for it.*

"Dana?"

"I guess we could work something out. I could talk to Frank and see if there's a slot in Cairo or Rabat. Which one do you think is closer?" Dana asked.

"Hell, I don't know. I don't exactly have my goddamned Rand McNally Road Atlas handy at the moment," Brownie snapped.

Jane had walked out on him two years earlier when he went to West Texas to drill oil wells, and she stayed in Oklahoma City. They stayed in touch by phone. And that was two years after Beatrice finally left him when he went to look for oil in Venezuela.

"Brownie, you're asking a lot," Dana said.

"I know. I know. But if we could..."

"Just screw around for a couple of years?"

"No. No, I didn't mean that. It's just..."

"What Brownie?"

"I just haven't had time to think this one through, you know. It just hit me."

"What about my parents and the ring?"

"I know. I know. I promised it to you, but that was before Aldair called me out of the blue. How was I to know?"

"Brownie? Make up your mind. Decide what you want and stick with it."

Not since the 504ᵗʰ Wing Commander had chewed him out for filing ten transfer requests in fourteen months (all denied), did Brownie feel he was under that much pressure.

Mildred came back with a warm-up shot to each of their cups. She slopped dribbles of coffee onto both of their saucers. Haute cuisine.

"Brownie?"

"I'm thinking." Thinking that maybe it was a mistake to get out of line and talk to her. Thinking that it was a bigger mistake to suggest that she come to Algiers. Thinking how angry Aldair would be once he found out that he had missed the plane for the third time in five days.

"Brownie?"

"Let's just go back to the hotel. Have a cocktail. Get a nice room. Let cooler heads prevail," he said.

"Brownie? We've done that two days in a row. What's it gonna be, mister?"

The shot-up B-17 skimmed just above the waves of the Mediterranean, one engine shut down, wind blowing through the torn-up flight deck, LaSuto spinning around and around in the top-turret searching for any glint of the ME-109 bloodsuckers that chased them, then lost them in the cloud cover. Gorman was still lead plane, and two of the four planes in the box-formation stayed with him. That way they had maybe 15-20 machine guns left to protect themselves.

"Are you sure this'll work, Brownie?" the navigator asked, *looping into and out of radio contact as they limped along.*

"Yeah, this guy from the 12ᵗʰ Bomb Group said they took a bead off the City of Marseilles, swung north and west over the Pyrenees, and then shot a fix almost due north for Plymouth, England."

"It's your call, Lieutenant. What do you want to do?" the navigator said.

"Brownie, what do you think?" Dana took his left hand into her right hand and smoothed it gently. Brownie was definitely weakening. He clenched his hand around hers in a firm grip and looked into those deadly dark-brown eyes.

"Brownie?"

"I make us out to have seven to ten minutes total flying time left. Gerry isn't anywhere near stupid enough to scramble fighters for a lone plane. Has anybody heard from Sultzmann in the ball turret?" the navigator asked.

"Brownie?" She's good-looking and we could have kids and a house with a white picket fence. And when she moans and caresses me, I just go all to pieces. Why don't you make up your mind you stupid shit? The last guy out of Stalag Luft 9, and the only one they couldn't crack in nine long months after capture.

"Sir, we're losing hydraulic fluids off the left wing, the tail is partially shot away, and the left forward aileron is flapping around like a ruptured goose."

"Brownie?"

"We should just sit down and work this all out. Dana, I just need a little more time."

"I'm showing #2 main is down to thirty-eight gallons, #3 has maybe thirty gallons, and #4 main has maybe twenty-five to thirty gallons left. Brownie, do you see any picket ships we could ditch next to? Are they ours?"

"Brownie?"

"I'm looking. I'm looking. I'm looking. I can just barely make out the shadows of something in the haze. Is that the cliffs or Land's End?

"Brownie?"

"I'm looking. I'm looking, goddammit. I'm looking as hard as I can, and I still don't see it."

Robert M. Pacholik

Robert M. Pacholik, a native of Chicago's Southside, served two combat tours in Vietnam as an Army field photographer and military journalist assigned to three commands during 1968 and 1969.

After completing his bachelor's degree, master's degree, and community college instructor credential at California State University, Sacramento, Pacholik worked on weekly, daily, and metro daily newspapers for ten years. In 1980, he went into the securities industry, where he spent twenty-nine years as a registered investment advisor, registered principal, and FINRA branch office manager. In the mid-1990s, Pacholik added teaching duties to his quiver. He taught in Sacramento, California, public and private universities including The University of Phoenix and California State University, Sacramento, for fifteen years.

Bob's first book, a military action adventure novel titled *Crab Louie: An Island Tale of Greed, Lust, and maybe Luv*, was published in August of 2012. The novel is set in the Caribbean, complete with an American offshore banker and a ruthless gun runner who wants to take control of the banker's $650 million bank.

Bob's second book, *Night Flares: Six Tales of the Vietnam War,* was published in April 2013 and won an MWSA Bronze Medal in 2014. His next book, *Crab Louie Deux*, a second military action adventure novel set in the Caribbean, is due out in mid-2016. He is now working on a murder mystery, set in 1968 Vietnam at the height of the war.

Bob and his wife, both now retired, live in Northern California, where he continues to scribble away.

38

TRIGGERS

Michael D. Mullins

Life placed me on a path that I didn't choose to rove.
That is not a complaint; I simply state a fact.
I often say I'm living a life I never even dreamed of.
We make choices hoping we sail the right tack
Along the way, but fate even directs who we love.
Much has been made of ships passing in the night.
We learn from each vessel below and above
And every crossing of a path changes our flight.

I have questions; I have doubts; my life is a quest.
I ask: "Who am I?" and "Why am I the way I am?"
There are no answers so all I can do is guess.
The person I am is a culmination of events in time.
Long ago, longer ago than ever I could predict,
I was sent to fight a little war, a conflict if you will,
In a small faraway country, equatorial and tropic,
And the ripples in that pond flow through me still.

I didn't start to write about PTSD, or any disability.
The opposite is true; that war showed me the way
Through life and from it I found a latent ability
To write and say things others can't always say.
I've asked if that was a gift or a plague a time or two.
The answer is always echoing in my mind ever so faintly.
"You are doing what you should be doing," says a voice.
I answer with, "Did I really have any other choice?"

A year in the jungle, the paddies, and the blazing sun
Rinsed occasionally by a torrential downpour, too,
I did what I was called to do, and would do it again,

Even with what I now know; I love the red, white, blue.
The words I heard when I came home, from foe and friend
Marked my spirit and charged something deep inside.
At times I laugh about those times way back then
And other times I can't help but hang head and cry.

It was a journey I took with eyes wide closed.
I think of hawks, eagles, and an occasional dove.
I regret nothing I did only doubting I did enough.
In moments of anger, not intentionally enflamed,
I still love my family, my friends, and all kinds of stuff.
When I resent how we were not permitted victory,
When I think about how many of us were defamed,
I wouldn't rewrite even one page of my story.

I walked into my first jungle a scared, young boy.
I walked out of it again as a scarred young man.
Scars are signs of healing, if you aren't destroyed.
I didn't know it at the time; it wasn't my plan,
Not knowing I was wounded, I buried things inside.
I lived, I loved, I worked long hours, tried to be a man.
It wasn't until many years later that I finally cried.
When my mind was free of the grind, I tried to understand.

War had actually shot a hole in my soul, what a shock,
To realize the things I'd said and done at times then
Made me a ticking clock, a seething bomb, tied in knots.
Some words set me off, authority was my enemy.
I resented being told what to do, being led by untried men.
Subconsciously I gauged things by an unspoken standard.
Had they done what I had done? Had they been where I was?
I found solace finally in the brotherhood of warriors then.

I don't intend to make excuses for bad behavior,
I was fighting my battle inside through the years.
I didn't give in to it, I conquered unspoken fears.
Drugs weren't my choice, I didn't self-medicate ever.
I worked, at work, in my community, I tried to live
In a way to make my father proud, live his standards.
I tried to be what my mother believed me to be.
I didn't know the journey was sprinkled with traps.

We veterans have to embrace what we did,
We have to dance with our demons, but lead.
When hands reach to us with compassion and love
We have to reach back and give them a chance
To help, to console, and teach them we are worthy.
We can't quit, we can't let ourselves be defined
By others, but take responsibility and help reshape
Our memories, forgive ourselves when we have doubt.

It took forty years to accept that the words
We read and heard about what we did can't be changed.
They are what they are, they were what they were.
Some of us came home, were belittled and estranged.
We didn't know what would become triggers for our
Malevolence, but it is our obligation to rearrange
The direction of our disappointment and realize
Too many don't get it, they'll never understand.

My soul isn't a piece of cloth; it can't be easily repaired.
I know now that the reception many of us experienced
Only made the hole in our souls bigger, triggering despair.
All the attention now, in movies and history, the welcome
Our newest warriors receive is the salve with which we heal.
All of it is both good and bad, makes us smile or come undone.
At times I cringe at the thought of watching another story
But I thank God they are more welcome and worthy of glory.

I wonder at times about the triggers I hear cocking.
Will I ever stop reacting with predictable antipathy?
When will I see things with anything akin to empathy?
If I ask others to understand, shouldn't I expect the same of me?
I don't want them to try to understand in reality.
To do so they must walk in my shoes; I want that for nobody.
I want only their acceptance and a modicum of respect
For me, my brothers and sisters in war, and our flag.

The questions will always be in my mind.
Can I identify the triggers, do I pull them myself?
Do those who oppose and disrespect us still
Pull the triggers with evil intent?
Do they love to say, "See, I told you so,
He or she is just another crazy warmonger?"
I'm strong enough at long last to tell them to take their best shot.
I know what I am and what I am not.

Join me in healing the scars, from conflict with bullets or words.
Heal yourself, believe in yourself, and lift yourself up.
Take help, want to change, take control of your destiny.
Fate lends a hand, directs us on a path,
But we make choices; we do make choices.
My questions may never be answered to my satisfaction,
But within us all waits reconciliation, pride,
And forgiveness; we did our duty.

Michael D. Mullins

Michael D. "Moon" Mullins is a Vietnam veteran, award-winning author and poet, and consummate storyteller. In March of 1968, Mullins was assigned to South Vietnam as a soldier in the 199th Infantry Brigade, where he served until March 1969. He was awarded the Purple Heart for wounds received in action during September 1968. After serving his country in Vietnam, Mullins earned a bachelor's degree from Clinch Valley College of the University of Virginia. Returning to his native Indiana with his wife, he completed a second undergraduate degree while working full time for a steel producer. Mullins retired in 2008 from Chrysler LLC where he was a supervisor/team leader.

Mike's first book was *Vietnam in Verse: Poetry for Beer Drinkers*, published in 2007. He followed that book with two more in 2011, co-authoring *Kings of the Green Jelly Moon* and authoring *Out of the Mist: Memories of War*. All three books have won awards. Mullins has also completed two award-winning audio books and an award-winning poster poem. Most recently Mullins co-authored *Pass the Salt, Doc* with Jim Greenwald, which was released in February 2013.

Mullins served as the vice president for Military Writers Society of America from 2009 to 2012. Married for forty-five years, he is the father of two sons and has six grandchildren. He was and is a believer in all that is good about the United States of America.

39

MAN OVERBOARD

David Michaelson

Some of my Army and Marine Corps friends claimed the Navy was an easy gig: no booby traps, no land mines, no snipers, and no bombs. Some of what they said is true, but not for the entire fleet, nor for every sailor. Sometimes things go wrong.

Ground troops have wartime advantages we swabbies don't have.There are no foxholes for shelter aboard ship, and no one ever sank to the bottom of a bomb crater filled with hungry sharks.

While I never served in combat during my five years in the Navy, we trained for it. We trained for all sorts of things including being bombed, strafed, and torpedoed. But it never happened, not to a submarine tender usually tied to a pier in San Diego. Fire is among the most feared shipboard incidents, followed closely by drowning. And we trained for both.

Losing a sailor while out at sea is something no one wants. "Man overboard!" is a desperate cry for help. The entire ship's company rallies around that call—a call to duty that can last for days—sometimes with success, sometimes not. We trained for that, too.

As Section One duty driver for the skipper, Captain Alan E. May, I was selected for a number of odd and unusual drills designed to hone our readiness for any emergency. One such drill required more hope and courage than I could have imagined.

In the middle of a massive and extremely powerful Pacific Ocean squall, where the waves crashed well above the O-2 decks, Captain May (nicknamed Big Al) decided to hold a realistic man overboard drill. He was known for realism.

For me, it all started during that vicious storm. We had been cooped up inside for a couple of days, portholes and hatches dogged down tightly. One stifling night, against regulations, I ventured out on deck for some fresh air. An unseen wave slammed into me, washing me aft with tremendous power. I grabbed frantically for stanchions and guardrail chains I knew were there, but couldn't see.

Finally, I was able to wrap one arm around a stanchion to arrest my imminent flushing into the black water. Between waves, I could see I had managed to snag the very last upright on that deck. But there was no hope and no courage involved with *that* particular act of stupidity. No, those more heroic things came the next day when Big Al secretly asked if I would be willing to portray a man overboard in the upcoming drill.

The plan was for me to sneak into a lifeboat before morning chow. No one was to know, not even my co-workers. Only the captain and the designated lifeboat crew knew of the plan.

Long before reveille, I sneaked under the tarp of that lifeboat and cuddled up next to a steel cage called a Stokes Litter. The litter is a wire basket in the shape of a human body which an injured, sick, or disabled person can be strapped into for safe transport.

It was dark in the lifeboat, but not cold, since we were in the tropics. I waited and waited. I could hear the shuffling of shoes as a few eager-beaver health nuts jogged around the ship. It was nearing 0800 hours and morning muster was in progress, but I wouldn't be there. I knew from past drills that my shipmates would be scouring the mess hall, the heads, and everywhere else before sounding the alarm.

Then it blared over the ship's loudspeaker system. "Man overboard! Man overboard! Man all duty stations. General quarters! This is *not* a drill." The dire warning was repeated several times. I could feel the mighty ship leaning hard to starboard as the lumbering tender began a wide 180-degree turn at flank speed—a whopping twelve or thirteen knots.

The lifeboat crew reported to Damage Control Central that they were in position to lower the boat. Suddenly it was light, as the heavy, black tarp was peeled back. A blanket was draped to hide me, just in case, and the three-man crew went about lowering the boat to the choppy water.

Once free of the lanyards and pulleys supporting the boat, the crew eagerly rowed off into the distance, as if directed to the location of a sailor who had fallen overboard sometime during the night.

Through a wind-whipped corner of the blanket I could see Captain May, his officers, and the sickbay medics standing by on the O-2 level. The ship was getting farther and farther away.

Now, I should point out that in my four years aboard ship I never suffered from seasickness, even when out to sea. That proud record was quickly coming to an end. The little boat was being tossed around like a cork. But as it turned out, nausea was not my biggest concern.

When the boat was completely hidden behind a monster wave, I was ordered to climb into the Stokes Litter. Being 6'4" and pushing 220 pounds, I found it to be a tight fit. The crew told me the captain wanted to make the rescue as realistic as possible, so they strapped me in and completely doused me with seawater. The captain had failed to mention either treatment.

On the way back to the ship, the little boat turned parallel to the waves, a very dangerous maneuver for any vessel. It's much safer to plow headlong into waves or with them—never broadside to them.

It was at that point, as the lifeboat rolled up on the face of another huge wave, that I looked straight down through my metal trap into Davey Jones's Locker. The boat, with me strapped into a steel cage, was upside down. In another second I would be falling into the deep, unable to move my arms or legs. It was a horrible, sinking feeling. The sea was angry, filled with foam and froth. I could see at least fifty feet down, the beams of sunlight penetrating the depths. I knew I would sink like an anchor. And for all I knew, the bottom was miles below. No one on this earth would be able to save me.

It was a life-changing moment for me. I look back upon that potentially deadly event with astonishment, for at the time, I was filled with hope and amazement—hope that the fragile little boat would right itself before I fell out, and amazement that I had the courage to volunteer.

After that episode, I extended my enlistment for one more year, just to see if the Navy would become my career.

It did not.

Foxholes are safer.

David Michaelson

David Michaelson served honorably in the United States Navy during the Vietnam era as a patternmaker aboard the USS *Sperry*, achieving the rank of E-5. His most memorable duty was that of section one duty driver for the flotilla's flag officer, a position that allowed much more freedom to leave the ship and go ashore on duty days. His unauthorized pizza runs were very popular with the crew.

At the age of eight, David began experimenting in the kitchen. Even though his earliest concoctions usually failed, he always returned to the kitchen. Eventually, he joined his local chef's association and filled the positions of events chair and treasurer. David has been a fill-in cook, a line cook, and an executive chef. He is a retired chef and restaurant owner, proudly boasting the fact that his Cozy Café was critically acclaimed for the food, the ambiance, and the service.

David has written fourteen novels, two cookbooks and a booklet on political satire. He is currently working on his memoirs. David's books have garnered many accolades from MWSA, including six medals, several recommended reading lists, and Author of the Month. He has been awarded a gold medal for his young reader's book, *Butterfly Dust*, and received silver medals for *The Burntwater Cook's Kitchen Guide* and *Rapscallion Summer*. Two Bronze medals complete the list.

David has been a professional umpire, a high school head volleyball coach, a USVBA volleyball player and referee, as well as a tournament handball player. He and his wife Dianne retired to rural Eastern Washington to pursue the craft of writing. David is an active member of the Patriot Guard Riders of Washington State.

40

RECOVERY

Jasmine Tritten

My life came to a complete stop in 1987 when a bicycle hit me while I walked in the bright sunshine on Girard Street in La Jolla, California. It happened during my lunch hour from the nearby gallery where I worked as an art consultant. I lay on the asphalt in a puddle of blood and ended up in the hospital with a deep cut in the back of my head, a severe concussion, and a broken tailbone.

When I opened my eyes, I found myself in a hospital bed. My head, wrapped in gauze, felt like it was going to burst like a balloon. And when I slowly lifted my head, the room began to spin around. Quickly I lowered it down again on the pillow. As I moved my legs, I felt an agonizing pain in my tailbone. Hurting all over and feeling completely trapped inside my body, I kept focusing on breathing in cold air through my nose and breathing out warm air through my mouth. This I learned in yoga classes, and it took away attention from my aching body.

"What happened to me?" I asked the doctor who stood next to my bed.

"A bicycle hit you," he said, bending over the railing.

"How and where?" I asked in shock.

"A young man raced on his bicycle, with the speed of a car, down a perpendicular street to Girard Avenue, where you walked. Out of control, unable to make the turn with the traffic, he jumped the curb onto the pavement, and knocked you down from the front." He continued, "You fell backwards and hit your head on the pavement with great impact."

"Oh my God!" Tears dropped down my cheeks and then I sobbed uncontrollably, because I hurt everywhere and felt so alone. My life was in jeopardy. I had left Carmel for a better job at the upscale art gallery in La Jolla to make more money, and now a year later, I was unable to move. Was this karma? Was there a lesson to be learned from this? I certainly had no clue. Maybe I needed not to focus on making money. Why did this happen?

Because of an extra long recovery time ahead, I was unable to get back to my glamorous job at the gallery and decided to return to Carmel where family and friends resided.

A dear pal volunteered to pick me up in La Jolla and drive me all the way back to the Monterey Peninsula with my stuff in the back of his covered truck, bless him. Grateful and sad at the same time, I waved goodbye to the challenging and stimulating life I experienced in the jewel of Southern California.

When I got home, friends right and left offered to help me get settled. Through close contacts, I found a beautiful room with my own bathroom and entrance in a house belonging to an elderly carpenter. Because of a knee operation and living alone, he needed immediate assistance. In exchange for the room, I got to tend an enormous vegetable garden and vacuum his house once a week. What a perfect way to heal my body and brain.

The house rested in raw nature next to the rippling Carmel Valley River. Sitting on a large stone next to the stream, I listened to water bubbling over rocks and watched trout climb up the rushing creek. To soothe my soul and spirit, I prayed and meditated in solitude under enormous eucalyptus trees.

Family and friends provided the love and emotional support I needed.

However, my depression continued. For the first time in my life, I succumbed to seeing a counselor. She told me the accident was considered a loss and I had not yet grieved the death of my alcoholic father when I was twelve years old. Until I processed that loss, I would be unable to resolve my current situation.

Stunned, I told my younger son Brendon of the sad discovery. He suggested, "Mom, how about going to one of the twelve-step programs? It's free and might help you."

Reluctantly I dragged myself to a twelve-step meeting for adult children of alcoholics. Not because I wanted to, but because I didn't want to disappoint my son. Through the whole session, I sat in a protective huddle with arms crossed, not saying a word. At the end of the meeting one of the attendees asked if anybody had a burning desire to share something before closing. In my heart, I knew that if I didn't tell them my story, I would never return.

So I raised my trembling hand and stood up to speak of my father's alcoholism and subsequent suicide. Words tumbled out of my mouth. Tears rolled down my cheeks. They handed me tissues. As I finished and sat down everybody in the room thanked me. I couldn't believe it! They all thanked me for sharing something I had been ashamed of all my life. I always thought if I told somebody what happened to my dad, they wouldn't like me. Instead, they expressed gratitude. Wow!

When I told Brendon about the meeting, he cheered, "Great, Mom! Try to go to three meetings in a row." Following his advice, I continued the meetings and learned to speak openly, sharing my feelings and thoughts with people I trusted. Tears kept flowing from my eyes for months. Since Dad's passing I had only cried on the inside. Finally, the tears seeped out of my body. At least I made progress. The sessions helped me to process my past trauma. If only these self-help programs had been around in Denmark when I grew up, my dad might have learned to cope with his alcoholism. He might have survived.

After numerous days of sitting by the flowing river in the afternoons, peace and harmony filled my soul and gave me strength, hope, and inspiration to start anew. Fate brought me back to Carmel Valley, into my inner self, where God resided.

The vegetable garden was bursting with greens. I enjoyed planting seeds, tending to the plants, and reaping the benefits later, sharing them with my landlord. Recovery was a slow process, but I improved day by day. My depression subsided. Light shined at the end of the tunnel. There was hope.

After receiving a lump sum of money from the insurance company of the guy who hit me, I bought a blue Hyundai car and a blue massage table. I signed up for classes in Carmel to become a massage therapist. While soothing and healing my injured head, I would be able to finally make money again. Somebody from above looked after me and guided me. Thank you! Thank you!

Jasmine Tritten

Jasmine Tritten grew up in Denmark and studied art in Europe from the time she was a young girl. In 1964, at the age twenty-one, she left her country for adventure on a big ocean liner from Copenhagen to New York. She ended up immigrating to the United States and settling on the Monterey Peninsula in California, where she obtained a degree in Interior Design. Jasmine met Jim Tritten, a professor at the Naval Postgraduate School in Monterey and they married in 1990. Later they moved to the East Coast where she received a Bachelor of Arts degree in Studio Art with a minor in English writing from Old Dominion University in Norfolk, Virginia.

Jasmine's second love is writing. She wrote journals since childhood and long letters to her mother in Copenhagen, who saved them in a large oak chest. Jasmine worked at Angel Press Publishers in Monterey, California, from 1984 to 1986, managing a bookstore, designing book covers, and helping edit books. In 1998, she had a poem published in *Tranquil Rains of Summer: The National Library of Poetry.* In 2013, she had "Mother's Day in Bolivia" published in *The Story- teller's Anthology: Presented by SouthWest Writers.* She had a children's story, "Kato's Grand Adventure," co-authored with her husband published in *Corrales Writing Group 2014 Anthology.* Her short story "Stumpy" was published in *Catching Calliope* Winter 2015.

Currently Jasmine is putting the finishing touches on her memoir, *The Journey of an Adventuresome Dane.* She resides in Corrales, New Mexico, with her husband and five cats.

41

LOSS OF INNOCENCE

Richard Davidson

Bobby and Billy were my close friends. They were brothers who might have been taken for twins, especially when they both wore their sailor suits. Bobby and I were in first grade together, while Billy was way up in third grade. One unique aspect of this school relationship was that while Bobby and Billy weren't twins, their teachers were. Our first grade teacher and Billy's third grade teacher, both named Miss Rask, were unmarried, redheaded, identical twin sisters.

After school, whenever we had time and permission, Bobby, Billy, and I would play together, frequently at their house instead of our three-room apartment. Their house was an old gray New England colonial type with a basement that included a no-longer-used coal bin, converted into a studio for their father, the first artist I ever met. He knew he had found an enthusiastic audience in me, and enjoyed showing me the basics of oil painting as well as his pet white mice.

Social norms were different in 1944, both because the background for our lives was the Second World War and because people respected authority and had no qualms about letting children run free. This was Boston, where even unaccompanied children traveled by bus and streetcar to local and special destinations and walked long distances to school and friends' homes and movie theaters.

One unusually warm and sunny autumn day, Bobby and Billy's father took them by bus to the Charles River near Harvard University, where he set up his easel to paint a view of the college while the boys played on the grassy, tree-lined bank of the river. It was a perfect day for almost any activity, and occasional lounging college students completed the tableau.

The boys played and raced along the riverbank for about an hour, attracting little attention. Then they discovered a treasure. Billy found some short boards, left over from a construction project. These would make perfect boats. Each brother took a board, and found a tree branch. Then they went to the edge of the river, where they each put a board into the water and shepherded it along the shore with a long tree branch.

This Navy game continued without incident for about fifteen minutes. Then Bobby's board boat floated out beyond the reach of his tree branch. He decided to wade in after it. The shock came when the water depth increased sharply, only two yards from the shore. Then he discovered that the peaceful appearance of the water's surface belied the strength of the river's current. Bobby yelled for help.

Billy looked around for adults, but saw none. He hesitated for what felt like forever. He knew he had to help Bobby; his dad had told him to take care of his younger brother. He didn't want to go into the river, but he knew he had to risk it. Billy shouted to Bobby that he was coming. He took his boat-herding branch into the water with him, hoping that Bobby would be able to grab it before the water got too deep. He waded, probed the bottom with his stick, and extended the stick toward Bobby. Then he waded, probed some more, and reached again. Then his feet could no longer touch the bottom.

The next day, Mom asked me to sit beside her on the couch. She showed me the newspaper, folded to show a particular article. Brothers drown in Charles River. I couldn't believe

I would never see them again. Bobby, Billy, and I had been inseparable friends, doing everything together. I cried for longer than I'd ever cried before as Mom held me in her arms. So this was the meaning of death—endless separation.

Richard Davidson

Richard Davidson is a former aerospace engineer who moved from government contracting to the commercial sector and then on to founding and developing a small firm, RADMAR, Inc. For more than forty years, this company created and manufactured audiovisual products, supplied specialized equipment and training materials for international aid applications, and performed media services on a contract basis. Within the past few years, RADMAR moved into publishing. All of these activities required the development and application of the decision-making principles described in Richard's book, *Decision Time! Better Decisions for a Better Life.*

Davidson is past president of Off-Campus Writers' Workshop and is the founder of the ReadWorthy Books book review blog. He is also a certified lay speaker in the United Methodist Church.

Richard is a long-time fan of British mysteries and presents lectures comparing the work of Agatha Christie and others with his own. He has written the five-volume Lord's Prayer Mystery Series: *Lead Us Not into Temptation*; *Give Us this Day Our Daily Bread*; *Forgive Us Our Trespasses*; *Thy Will Be Done*; and *Deliver Us from Evil*. His current project, The Imp Mysteries, has so far produced *Implications*, which weaves together actions occurring in multiple time periods, and *Impulses,* which involves several accidental and suicidal deaths that aren't what they appear to be, plus paranormal events based on true case studies.

42

THE HUNT

Brian Wizard

During the Viet Nam War, I was a permanent door gunner on the smokeship *Pollution IV*. This unique combat assault helicopter had an all-volunteer crew, as flying on it was considered to be "beyond the call of duty." *Pollution IV* had three door gunners, with one also being the crew chief. We sat on fifty gallons of fired-retarded oil held in a container beneath the middle seat. When needed, the aircraft commander (AC) would engage the electric pump that would inject the oil through jets mounted on a circular smoke ring into the turbine exhaust. The spray of oil would immediately turn into a blinding white smoke.

Our main mission was to protect the flight of nine troop-carrying helicopters by leading the way into the area of operation's landing zone during a combat assault into enemy territory. Our smokescreen prevented the enemy gunners from taking aim on the helicopters flaring to a stop so the troops could disembark.

The insertion of troops never took long, so between insertions we would go on what my pilot called *the hunt*.

I flunked my flight physical due to colorblindness. That being the only problem I had, the doc said, "It's your ass." Good thing, too, as during one of our hunting missions we made an "accidental" excursion into the neutral and sovereign country of Cambodia. I noticed some movement of people, distinct bunker emplacements that made up a perimeter, and a thriving enemy encampment about a mile out at my two o'clock position. I mentioned this to my pilot,"We have some serious activity at our two o'clock."

The AC turned the ship in that direction and lowered its nose to see what I was talking about, thus lowering the ship on a collision course with the suspected enemy encampment.

My voice may have risen in pitch when I reiterated what I was seeing, "We have enemy troops very much on the move now. Do you see it, right there at our twelve o'clock?"

"No," the pilot replied, as he was not colorblind and the enemy's camouflage worked fine on him. Panic struck my heart as we continued to lower into the active enemy area. "Do you see it *now*?" were my last words before I started shooting, as I could no longer wait for permission, instruction, or command.

"It's a damn NVA base camp," the AC finally responded, as soon as he had us so close he could not help seeing the activity through the camouflage.

What made *Pollution IV*'s AC the champion of all ACs, in my opinion, is that he knew when to turn and run and when to push all bets into the center of the table and fight to the finish. In an all-or-nothing maneuver, he dropped *Pollution IV* into a low-level flight across the NVA base camp from one side of the perimeter to the next, instructing his gunners to "kill them all." We smoked our way across the fortified enemy stronghold at a hundred-plus knots, with our M-60 machine guns hammering hard at every enemy we could nail.

I shot into the crowds of running soldiers, into subterranean bunker doorways, and I especially remember seeing three NVA soldiers in the upcoming perimeter bunker. I am sure they were totally surprised at our daring race across what they considered very safe territory. My machine gun's bullets plunged into their open pit bunker, hitting two, with the third taking cover as we passed over.

The battle didn't stop once we were beyond the enemy base camp's perimeter. We flew high into the sky, circling the base camp. Our fifty-caliber machine gun lobbed bullets into the NVA base camp with gravity on our side. The NVA fired their fifty-one caliber bullets up at us, with gravity working against them, and we watched with delight as their tracer bullets failed to reach our altitude.

Meanwhile, the AC worked out the coordinates of the base camp's exact location, radioed the Air Force, and asked for some aerial fire support. A loaded B52 bomber responded, telling us to clear the area ASAP, as he was only five minutes out, which is like being there already.

I sat with my 35mm camera in the ready position and took this next photo of the base camp lifting 1500 feet into the air as it turned into dust particles created by the massive bomb strike.

Needless to say, it was an amazingly great day of combat, since I lived to write about it. Of course, this unauthorized event never happened and this photo doesn't exist. The real rub was how we weren't allowed the very substantial body count for our actions.

This is the smoke ring of the vintage smoke generator I located, purchased, and donated to the Smithsonian National Air and Space Museum, Chantilly, Virginia. It is installed on a Huey that has a history of being a smokeship, and presently on display, along with my custom-painted flight helmet and platoon scarf.

[Excerpted from the award-winning photo book Smokeships Always Leading the Way. Photo credits: Roger Connor, Brian Wizard, Dave Norton, Dave Evans]

Brian Wizard

Brian "Wizard" Willard has done a lot of post-war work documenting his combat experience in the Viet Nam War and shares it through his books, *Permission to Kill, Back in the World, Permission to Live, Pollution IV, Smokeships Always Leading the Way*, and best of all, through his DVD documentary, *Viet Nam: Then, Again, and Beyond*, which won Best Documentary (short) in the New York Indie Film Festival in 2005. The DVD has three major segments: *Thunderhawks*, composed of actual combat footage shot from the door of Pollution IV; *Make Friends Not War*, a cathartic return to Viet Nam in 1999, and *Smokeships Always Leading the Way*, the dedication of the vintage smoke generator Brian donated to the Smithsonian Institute National Air and Space Museum in Chantilly, Virginia. Three original music videos are also on the DVD.

Brian Wizard has penned eight other novels: *Shindara, Heaven on Earth*, the Space Egg Trilogy, *Space Hunts*, and two true crime novels, *Game Over!* and *Don't be Scammed*, depicting his efforts as a private contractor to thwart the success of the Nigerian global financial terrorism we all receive via email as scams. Four of Brian's books and his Viet Nam DVD have won awards for their excellence. His counter-fraud efforts have saved countless scam victims worldwide.

43

LAUNCHING A LEGACY

Martha J. LaGuardia-Kotite

May 17, 2015

A tug nudged then pushed forcefully into the starboard bow of the U.S. Coast Guard Cutter *Hamilton*. A second one approached, pressing into her stern quarter. Lines tossed from the tug's deckhands were securely fastened to the ship. It was 12:35 p.m., the first Saturday in November. For six months, the men and women assigned to the *Hamilton* prepared for this day. One of the service's newest Legend-class National Security Cutters, these frigate-sized vessels play a vital role in the U.S. Coast Guard's strategy to combat transnational organized crime, secure borders, and safeguard commerce as far from our shores as possible.

This resource is in great demand. The cutter's speed, robust C4ISR (command, control, communication, computers, intelligence, surveillance and reconnaissance) equipment are powerful instruments for international partnerships, defense readiness, and border security. Complemented by fast small boats the vessel can launch helicopters from her decks.

The special sea detail was set. The Coast Guardsmen took their assigned positions on the bridge, in the Command Information Center, on deck, and in the engine room. Six mooring lines were methodically removed from the pier's cleats and snaked aboard. At 1:15 p.m., the rock band Styx's hit song

"Come Sail Away," blared over the ship's loudspeakers and a stiff breeze carried the tune ashore. A bridge watch stander piped, "Thank you, Huntington Ingalls. Next stop Charleston."

Hamilton's legacy is launched. A lot has changed in ship design and capability since the last Hamilton namesake cutter launched over forty years ago. Forged from mountains of steel carefully cut, placed, and welded together over three years, now, a community of men and women proudly leave the shipyard, the first to serve aboard the cutter. These 119 people are exclusively known as plank owners—those who brought this 418-foot ship Huntington Ingalls built, to life. As plank owners, they face unique challenges preparing the vessel to depart its birthplace and safely sail her home to Charleston, South Carolina, to be commissioned, placed in active service, on December 6, 2014.

In order to cast off the mooring lines that secured this floating town to land and transition from the safety of a shore to sea, each plank owner is assigned a job in one of the departments: combat systems, operations, engineering, or support. As a team, they share the responsibilities and challenges of preparing this cutter for her maiden voyage home and completing a ready for sea certification. Within twelve months they must also demonstrate that the vessel is ready for operations. They are men and women, aged nineteen to fifty-five years old, hailing from Hawaii to Maryland.

The ship's commanding officer, Captain Doug Fears, bears the brunt of the responsibility. He's from Maryland's eastern shore. He says there's a euphoric phase in settling into the role of captain. The honeymoon fades quickly when reality sets in with shipyard demands. Fears focuses on his looming deadline to accept the ship. With the help of his crew, he has to certify, like inspecting a new car, whether *Hamilton* is ready to roll off the lot to begin her decades of service on the seas.

To prepare, Fears sits down with each crewmember, getting to know them. "We are shipmates for life," Fears explains. "Call on me anytime now or in the future. What can I do for you?" In return, he tells his crew, "I want your excellence." He says, "It cuts both ways."

The pre-commissioning of a National Security Cutter is new for everyone. The 42-year-old head chef, Senior Chief Petty Officer Traci Addicott, starts from scratch. Although this is her fifth ship and her 22nd year in the U.S. Coast Guard, Addicott says, "We're all green. I don't think that happens too often in the Coast Guard. I've never established a galley before and to do it within a year...this is a once in a lifetime event."

As the Food Services Division Officer, she supervises a team of eight men. They sanitize the galley and mess deck, fill refrigerators and freezers, stocks supplies, spices and cooking utensils. She plans menus to accommodate people with allergies or vegan diets.

"Three times a day, I've got 110 to 120 mouths to feed," she says, rattling off a shopping list like it was a verse to her favorite song. For one week, serving meatloaf and tacos, she needs sixty pounds of ground beef per meal. Every week 120 pounds of bananas are consumed. "They're good eaters. These kids are drinking chocolate milk twice as fast as white milk—ten gallons a day." She muses aloud, "Food is the biggest morale on the ship."

From Brookfield, Ohio, Addicott fills the role of Senior Enlisted Advisor relaying crew concerns to the captain. According to Fears, she's the mayor. "I tell everybody to come talk to me," Addicott says.

Positive crew morale and food is important, especially when a typical patrol will run sixty to ninety days. Living and working in the confined areas, the crew bonds, becoming shipmates, developing a "tight-knit camaraderie" says Chief

Warrant Officer 2 J.P. Michaud. He grew up in Fort Walton Beach, Florida. After seven consecutive years afloat, he asked for assignment on the *Hamilton*, he says, because of the crew. "On land there's more of a division between divisions. The only thing I don't like is the lack of windows." To look out of one, Michaud has to climb to the bridge from his workplace in the engine room where he keeps the main engines running.

It's 2 p.m. Nearly an hour and a half after leaving the shipyard, Hamilton is eleven nautical miles away, cruising in the Gulf of Mexico on her own. Dolphins play in her bow wake. The nearly 4,500-ton vessel rides smoothly through the six-foot seas like a Cadillac on the interstate. In cruising mode, at thirteen knots, this is merely half her top speed. To get where Commander Steve Matadobra, the executive officer from Brooklyn, New York, calls "serious-ass speed," the gas turbine is combined or connected to the two diesel engines, powering and spinning the shafts, propelling the vessel to twenty-eight knots.

Hamilton eases to ten knots. Four-hour watches are set throughout operational and mechanical areas. In the engine room, Petty Officer 2nd Class Christine Doggett stands the evening watch. From Glendale, Arizona, she enlisted ten years ago, before getting married and having three sons, Roland, Rhue, and Raine, all now under five years old.

Before reporting to *Hamilton*, she worked at Coast Guard Station Manistee tucked on the eastern shore of Lake Michigan. "Can't sit behind a desk," Doggett says. While she learned a lot about ship engines, her job on *Hamilton* is an apprenticeship.

"My challenge is everything," she says of Hamilton's multi-level engine room. "I'm starting to get a grasp on it."

One of Hamilton's twenty women (seventeen percent of the crew are female), Doggett is pleased to serve with what she says is an unusual number of women on a ship. Five of the females work in the engineering department with thirty men. Doggett stands out for her dedication and for the colorful fantasy dragons tattooed on her arm. She says they represent her. They "are strong, powerful, majestic. They can still be beautiful and tough at the same time." With a big smile, she says, "I don't do snarling dragons."

When the sun rises, so does the crew.

Pensacola is the first stop, then Miami where they will host a reception. Addicott plans appetizers for 100 guests, including the Commandant of the U.S. Coast Guard. "It's going to be fine," Addicott says. "I've done a million of these."

Then, *Hamilton* will turn left rounding the tip of Florida, her sleek, steel hull cutting through the Atlantic Ocean. She is coming home.

Photo by Martha LaGuardia-Kotite

Martha LaGuardia-Kotite

Martha LaGuardia-Kotite is a journalist, author, mom, and professional speaker with public relations and military experience. A graduate of the U.S. Coast Guard Academy, Martha served two tours at sea aboard the USCGC *Resolute* Oregon, and as executive officer of the USCGC *Padre* in Key West, Florida. After ten years of active duty she served as a reserve officer for an additional fifteen years, including service as press secretary for the Commandant of the U.S. Coast Guard. Martha holds a master's degree in journalism from Harvard University Extension School and has published features in magazines as well as a cover story in the *Boston Globe*.

Martha enjoys writing about extraordinary adventures and challenging topics, with which she hopes to make a difference through awareness and inspiration. The greatest joys she has received from her work are invitations to lend her experience to talk about leadership, leaning on her military service insights, as a keynote speaker for schools, book clubs, and professional organizations or corporations.

Martha has written four books: *So Others May Live: Coast Guard Rescue Swimmers Saving Lives, Defying Death*; *Changing the Rules of Engagement: Inspiring Stories of Courage and Leadership from Women in the Military* and most recently a tribute to the power and presence of our national flag *My Name Is Old Glory*. *So Others May Live* won four awards including a gold medal from MWSA. This year she will publish a children's book about successful people in Science, Technology, Engineering, and Mathematics (STEM) careers.

Photo by Martha LaGuardia-Kotite

44

FOR THE FOLKS
BACK HOME

Gary A. Best

December 7, 1943 to December 6, 1944

The scrapbook was filled with newspaper reports that we were knocked down, that we were shot down, and that we were sunk. But it also contained the words that the folks back home wanted to read and believe: that we were able to get up, take to the air again, and cover the oceans with a rebuilt armada.

It was buried under a pile of stuff in the treasures-to-trash, jewels-to-junk venue common to the American institution of weekend parking lot excess: The Sunday Swap Meet. Who had made the scrapbook of newspaper clippings from World War II is not identified on any of its pages nor is the name of the newspaper from which the precisely snipped and preserved headlines and story columns were taken.

Why was this digest of war news started on December 7, 1943, two years after that horrible day that will live in infamy? Was this a part of a collection of multiple year compilations or perhaps a snapshot of what the folks at home read while their son, father, or other family member or friend served in the military? The scrapbook contained multiple entries for each day for one year, the words carefully selected to stir hope for the future and spell out the courage that would be needed by everyone who read about the progress and setbacks of the war.

The selections below from the scrapbook's collection represent reports from each month of the reporting year, a year of hope and courage. All are from the scrapbook and are exact quotes with some editing for length to accommodate this anthology. Entries in all capital letters represent newspaper headlines.

December 7, 1943: Germany's Defeat in 1944 Foreseen

December 14, 1943: Allies Pierce Jap Lines Expanding Pacific Offensive

December 25, 1943: Yule Finds Allies on Offensive at All Fronts in Pacific

December 26, 1943: THE GREAT ALLIED aerial offensive against Germany, and Nazi-dominated Europe, culminating in smashing blows at the French channel coast, highlighted the war news this week.

January 3, 1944: Berlin Raided Heavily Twice in 24 Hours. Berlin, the R. A. F.'s first target for 1944, was given its second seething bath of fire and bombs of the New Year today by British airmen. The blow cost 28 bombers; Resistance stiff.

January 14, 1944: Japs Mowed Down in "Prepare to Die" Attack on Marines. For fully five minutes the Japanese charged and shouted, "Prepare to die, marines." At 4:15 a.m. they charged. Five times they charged, and five times the United States marines hurled them back in what has become the fiercest battle of the Cape Gloucester campaign, the battle of Walt's Ridge.

January 27, 1944: Supplies Pour Ashore; Rome Wedge Wider. The first German counterattack against the Americans and British just south of Rome, the first of the many that probably will be launched in a furious effort to wipe out the

Allied beachhead, has been thrown back with the crushing of German armor.

January 28, 1944: Thousands of Prisoners Die from Brutality. Army-Navy disclosure of heart-sickening mistreatment of the gallant defenders of Bataan and Corregidor at the hands of their Japanese captors was followed quickly today by an official promise to bring those responsible to account.

February 7, 1944: Nazi Bombers Blast Allied Bridgehead; American Nurses Among victims in Vicious Blow; Street Fighting Still Going on in Cassino Area.

February 16, 1944: R.A.F. Drops 2800 Tons by 800 to 900 heavy bombers; 43 lost. The R.A.F. smashed Berlin last night with the greatest load of bombs ever dropped on a single target.

February 25, 1944: Nazi Air Force Now Fighting for Existence; Allies Striving for Knockout Punch in Skies.

March 25, 1944: Yanks Cut Off Jap Retreat in North Burma. Merrill"'s Marauders in north Burma have captured Shaduzup and cut off the retreat of Japanese being pushed southward down the Mogaung Valley.

March 29, 1944: American Flying Fortresses plunged deep into central Germany today and Liberators pounded the Pas-de-Calais coastal area of France in the campaign described officially as aimed primarily against the Luftwaffe on the ground and in the air.

April 11, 1944: Record Bomb Load Dropped in Night Blow. Nearly 2,000 American bombers and fighters, following up a record 4000-ton attack by the R.A.F., carried the onslaught against German air defenses through its fourth day today with assaults against plane factories at Oscherslesen and Bernburg and other targets deep in Germany.

May 3, 1944: MAJORITY OF MEATS OFF RATIONING LIST

June 5, 1944: Remnants of Two German Armies Flee. The powerful Fifth Army thundered across the Tiber toward northern Italian horizons in pursuit of the 10th and 14th German Armies today.

June 6, 1944: BROAD FRENCH FRONT ESTABLISHED BY ALLIES. The Allies landed in the Normandy section of northwest France early today and by evening had smashed their way inland on a broad front, making good a gigantic air and sea invasion against unexpectedly slight German opposition.

June 7, 1944: Greatest Air Armada Aids in Invasion. Allied air forces taking supreme command of the air over invaded France flew well over 13,000 sorties from dawn yesterday until dawn today.

June 11, 1944: ALLIES OPEN 2ND STAGE OF EUROPEAN INVASION

June 16, 1944: Gigantic New Planes Strike Nip Homeland. Four of America's mighty sky battleships (the B-29) were lost in yesterday's attack on Yawata, the "Pittsburgh of Japan."

June 19, 1944: Germany's rocket bomb assaults on southern England continued for the fifth consecutive day as a number of the fire-spitting, jet-propelled robot planes zoomed across the coast just after daybreak today.

July 1, 1944: Narrowing of the Allied forces' semicircle around the Japanese homeland has stepped up the fury of the enemy's ground defense.

July 5, 1944: Hitler Grim in Plea for Production. Adolf Hitler, in the grimmest speech of his career, warned today that Germany is fighting for its very existence and acknowledged that the Allies have far outstripped the Reich in war production.

July 6, 1944: German robot bombs concentrated upon London have killed 2,752 persons and sent 8,000 to hospital in the last three weeks.

July 14, 1944: Superfortress Crews Victims of Savage Foe. Japanese radio broadcasts today were heard reporting the execution of several captured B-29 crew members and threatened that "any Allied airman who falls or bails out over Japan will be executed."

July 20, 1944: Fuhrer Hurt Slightly by Bomb Blast. Berlin announced that Adolf Hitler was burned and bruised in an unsuccessful bombing attempt on his life today.

August 4, 1944: Nippon Empire Cracks Along Conquest Line. Japan's conquest-swollen empire is ripping badly at the seams in India, Burma, the Marianas, and New Guinea.

August 22, 1944: PATRIOTS LIBERATE PARIS. Southern Front Push Ahead of Schedule; Germans in "Rout" on Lower Seine River

September 13, 1944: SIEGFRIED LINE PIERCED. American doughboys invading Germany have captured Rotgen, nine miles southeast of the stronghold of Aachen, and stormed tonight against pillboxes and anti-tank obstacles.

September 17, 1944: Landings Made After Furious Shell Attacks; MacArthur Says "Defeat Stares Japan in Face."

October 20, 1944: MacArthur, Keeping Vow to Come Back, calls on the people of the archipelago to "rise and strike" their Japanese conquerors.

November 8, 1944: ROOSEVELT WINS, TAKES MAJORITY OF CONGRESS

December 6, 1944: The last entry in the scrapbook, one year after it was started: Still Not Free.

Gary A. Best

Gary A. Best holds a doctorate from the University of Minnesota and has written and traveled extensively in his professional field, lecturing abroad and living and teaching in Taiwan as a Senior Fulbright Scholar. He is the recipient of the Outstanding Professor Award from his university and has been named a distinguished alumnus of two colleges.

Gary's first book outside of his professional field was published in the United States and the United Kingdom and is an MWSA medalist: *Belle of the Brawl: Letters Home from a B-17 Bombardier.* His second nonfiction work about World War II, *Silent Invaders: Combat Gliders of the Second World War,* has been published in the United Kingdom. Gary's first work of fiction, a story about a crew of a B-17 bomber during World War II, is titled *Tink's Tank* and was published in December 2014.

When not pounding on a keyboard and developing more stories, Gary and his wife like to travel. Gary has visited all seven continents since his retirement in February of 2002, and his wife has been to six, saying, "I don't do cold." Gary's favorite trips to date are Antarctica where the ice is amazing, a Kenyan/Tanzanian safari, a polar bear expedition to Churchill on the Hudson Bay, and Australia where the colors of the Great Barrier Reef defy description.

Photo of Scrapbook Cover, courtesy of Gary A. Best

Scrap Book

45

ALZHEIMER'S

Karl Boyd Hoepfner

My wife of 58 years, Carol, is a retired master sergeant from the United States Air Force. The courage, hope, and determination she has shown throughout the stages of her life are extraordinary.

I wrote this poem to let her know that regardless of what happens in the future, there is always hope that some day we will meet again and love as we have for all these wonderful years.

It is also my hope that this poem will inspire those who are caretakers of their loved ones. I share their pain, and this was one way to ease mine.

For Carol

You're here,
But you're not.
Although I may see you 24 hours
Of each and every day,
I still miss you a lot,
Since your mind has gone astray.
Your body is in that chair,
Over there,
But your mind is out in space;

Somewhere...
And after 58 years together,
You know that I still care.

They say we have a Lord to always be our friend,
But I find it so very hard to comprehend,
Why murderers and rapists get pardoned,
But a good woman like you He can't mend.
Does that make sense to you, my dearest friend?

When you wake in the middle of the night
With a bad dream you can't understand,
I hold you tight, lie, and say it's all right,
And rub your neck and your back with my hand,
As I kiss your hair to try to ease your fright.

You talk to others at night
Your sisters and children I can't see,
But hush, everything's all right;
I'm still here, it's just me.

Once I was your lover, husband,
Companion, friend, and world-shaker,
With a love that would never ever bend,
But now I'm just your "caretaker."
But I still can hold your hand
And share a love that will never end.

Thank God before all this happened,
We saw the world with all its charms,
Each day after lovely day.
While our nights were always so splendid,

With you in my arms,

We danced all our cares away.

Yes, we have cruised to all seven continents,

Saw things that we never thought we would see.

It was always just the two of us, me and you,

But that was all right; we were always content,

Just being you and me.

We have traveled to so many cities,

In sunshine, but sometimes there was a little rain.

(And I must admit we sang some ditties,

While neither of us was feeling any pain).

But how could we know it was a pity,

We would never sail smooth seas again.

One day a rare form of cancer decided to come calling;

And took away all of your sight.

But I still hear your tears as they are falling,

On your pillow late at night.

And I know that you are crying for our kids and the family,

But mostly you are thinking of how things used to be.

As if that wasn't enough, atop it all,

Alzheimer's decided to pay you a call.

You've always been a fighter, so you responded well,

And fought your way bravely through

your own personal hell.

Against that dreaded disease your attitude

was always swell.

But now I can see that you are slipping,

Just a little bit more each day,

As Alzheimer's keeps on chipping,

Away at your memory,

And attempting to have its way.

But there are some spells,

When the fog will vanish,

Like spooks just after Halloween,

And your mind will seem so clear.

That's when you say, "I love you,"

And often call me "Dear."

But though I try like hell

I just can't seem to banish,

These mind-ghosts from the scene.

They lurk there beneath the surface,

And remain there, unable to be seen,

To fill your heart, and mine, with dread.

(God grant me absolution,

For wishing it was me instead.)

This dreadful disease,

Just never seems to ease.

Once you were never blue,

But now you're not pleased,

With anything that I do.

But I continue as I can,

Doing what I know how to do.

Sometimes because you can't see,

You don't even know it's me,

But think I'm just a man,
That takes good care of you.

I feed, bathe, and dress you,
Brush your teeth and comb your hair.
Your smile says you like what I do,
While your mind doesn't seem to care.
It's off on another journey, and I'm not invited along.
I hope it's a place to put a smile on your face,
Filled with laughter, love, and a song.

Already knowing your fate,
All I can do is wait,
For that terrible date when you will depart,
This earth for a heavenly state.
That's when I will lose my soul mate,
And my heart.

But don't worry when you are gone,
And I am left here all alone,
For you see, I won't really be,
You'll always be here with me.
In my mind and my heart,
We will never truly be apart.

Some will remember you after you've gone away,
While others shall soon forget.
But every minute of every day,
Who will mourn and love you, and think of you yet?

Friends or Family? Mostly.
An old adversary? Probably.

But positively and forever until eternity
And beyond the sun and sea,
There will always be:
Me!

Carol Hoepfner, Karl's wife

Karl Boyd Hoepfner

Karl Boyd Hoepfner (who writes under the pen name of Karl Boyd), resides with his wife of 58 years, Carol, in the sleepy fishing village of Rockport, Texas. Both are retired master sergeants from the United States Air Force.

Karl is the author of *Terroristic Signs*; *From China with Love*; *Palmyra, Isle of Death*; *The Lost Priest*; and the four-part mystery series comprised of *The Nearly Perfect Plan*, *The Cyrus Caper*, *The Texas Two Card Hold 'em Heist*, and *The Don's Stimulus Package*.

Due to his submission of a 400-word essay explaining why they should be declared the winners of Whataburger's national search, Karl and Carol were awarded the title of Whataburger's Biggest Fans. They used $7,000 of their prize money to purchase meals for 1,000 homeless and needy people while they conducted a tour of 738 Whataburger stores in ten states. In August of 2012 at the end of their trip, they received a proclamation from Texas Governor Rick Perry and the keys to a brand new Chrysler Town and Country van from Whataburger CEO Hugh Dobson.

Karl and Carol's story has been featured on *Oprah, The Today Show*, and more than 200 television stations and in 300 newspapers nationwide including the *Air Force Times* and *London Daily Mail*.

Karl is currently penning a sequel to *Terroristic Signs* entitled *The Last Adversary* and is also looking forward to the 2015 winter publication of a Christmas poem/illustrated book *Ralph the Tallest Elf*, which can be viewed on his blog, Karl's Korner.

46

THE KISS THAT LAUNCHED A NOVEL

Arlene Eisenbise

In 1995 as the fiftieth anniversary of the end of World War II approached, an article appeared in the *Green Bay Press-Gazette*. I was employed by the Social Security Administration in Green Bay, Wisconsin, at the time and occasionally wrote articles on assignment for their newspaper.

A woman claiming to be the nurse in the famous Alfred Eisenstaedt photograph, known as the V-J Day kiss, had come forward. The search for the kissing sailor took off. Many men claimed to be "the one." Hadn't every sailor been kissing someone on the day that President Truman announced the end of the four-year war?

The former nurse tested several of the claimants, surrendering to their back-breaking embraces and deep kisses. She ruled out several based on memory. I'm not convinced that a fifty-year-old kiss can be remembered that clearly, but I may be wrong.

One Glenn McDuffie set out to prove that he was the sailor in the famous photo. On that celebrated day in 1945, he had just exited a subway entrance on Times Square in New York City when he heard the President's announcement. Exhilarated by the news, Glenn grabbed a nurse he spotted standing in the street, bent her backwards over his arm, held her in a neck hold, and planted the famous kiss on her lips. McDuffie felt so confident of his claim that he spent more than sixty years attempting to prove that he was the sailor in the famous photo, including telling everyone that he met.

Glenn's final effort made his story more believable. He contacted Lois Gibson a police sketch artist in Houston, Texas. She took nearly a hundred photos of Glenn in his kissing position. By layering the original Eisenstaedt photo with those she took of McDuffie, Gibson became convinced. The muscle and bones matched, but most convincing for her was his ear, which Gibson claimed to be "the most complicated thing on your head." Glenn's ear was an exact match to that of the sailor in the V-J Day kiss photo. He lived to the age of eighty-six, content that he had proven his place in history.

The V-J Day kiss story had planted a seed, and I considered writing about my own war-time experience. Three years later during a visit with my cousin Ray (Bud) Bowers in Oregon, I mentioned my idea to write about life in an overflowing trailer camp near Milwaukee, Wisconsin, during the 1940s.

Unlike so many World War II veterans who buried their stories, Bud shared his unique end-of-war experience. He was one of my eight cousins who served in that war. By some miracle, all of them escaped major injury.

Peace documents had been signed in September 1945, but Bud had not yet returned home from overseas. I remember the waiting. Christmas was around the corner, family was worried, and communication was censored.

As Bud related being sent to Nuremburg ahead of the start of the war trials, I took copious notes. My cousin had served as a sharpshooter. The original plan had been to have a firing squad carry out the punishment of the war criminals. Bud and the others were not informed of the exact nature of their assignment. They didn't know why they were in Nuremberg until the prisoners—including Herman Goering, Rudolph Hess, and Karl Doenitz—began to arrive. Bud was often handcuffed to one or the other of them. He conversed with them and even taunted Hess.

"You know Hitler has you down as AWOL," Bud teased Hess because of his mysterious flight to Scotland in May of 1941.

Finally it was decided to release the firing squad and to bring in a hangman to render the punishment when the trials ended. Bud was excited about possibly making it home by Christmas. The war prisoners overheard our soldiers' discussions. Many of the Nazis were superstitious, intrigued by the occult—everything and anything that might aid their winning the war. Doenitz—named as the Fuehrer's successor following Hitler's alleged suicide—warned about crossing the Atlantic during the winter months. Better to wait until spring, he advised; the worst storm in years was predicted for the Atlantic.

But who was prepared to listen to the enemy? During his journey aboard ship, as the storm raged, and the men bailed water, Bud recalled those words of warning.

For security reasons, soldiers destined to return to the States left from staging areas labeled as cigarette camps, named for brands of American cigarettes. The camp that Bud departed from was named Camp Lucky Strike. The ship and its passengers needed all the luck they could get during their harrowing journey across the angry Atlantic in late 1945.

With the war over, and having been away from loved ones for four torturous years, servicemen were eager to return to the States any way they could. The ship Bud was assigned to, the *Portland,* included a hangar for Corsair planes—those designed with folding wings. The hangar was returning empty. Many medics eager to leave the war behind asked to sleep in the hangar to speed their return home. During the predicted storm at sea, an antennae collapsed on the hangar. Sadly, many more lives were lost. The ship was required to turn back to the Azores to drop off the bodies. That, Bud said, was when he realized that war losses did not necessarily end when the last enemy bullet was fired.

All seeds need germinating and Bud's stories began the germination process for my novel. What began as a chuckle about a stolen kiss fifty years earlier, developed into a young-adult historical book.

My main goal as I worked on the writing over the years was to see *Big War, Little Wars* published during Bud's lifetime. In August of 2014—a month following my book's publication date—I traveled to Oregon to deliver a personalized copy to Ray (Bud) Bowers. He was then a spry ninety-one years old. He admired his young image on the cover and kissed my cheek. That was a proud and rewarding moment for both of us.

He was, and is, the last of our family's eight World War II survivors still among us.

Arlene Eisenbise

Wisconsin native, Arlene Eisenbise studied creative writing, freelance writing, and literature at the University of Wisconsin, Stevens Point, at the School of the Arts at Rhinelander, and at The Clearing in picturesque Door County.

She is the mother of five successful adult children who call five different states home.

Arlene writes novels that allow her fictional characters to experience historical events for educational and entertainment purposes. Her articles about the arts, travel, and home décor appeared in Wisconsin's leading newspapers.

She became an Indie Author in the summer of 2014 with the release of her young adult historical novel, *Big War, Little Wars—a story for all ages.* Her poetry has appeared in three *Barney Street editions—VIII, IX, and XII—*published by the University of Wisconsin – Stevens Point, and with *Wisconsin History in Poetry.* A short story was featured in *Writing Raw,* an e-zine.

Arlene has been an active member of the Society of Children's Book Writers and Illustrators since 1994 and a long-time member of the Professional Writers of Prescott, having served as their Vice-President for three years.

Arlene diverted her desire to play the piano to the challenge of another keyboard—believing it a wise choice—since the piano keyboard features neither cut nor paste. She now resides in sunny Arizona, where she continues to imagine and to write.

47

COURAGE, AND HOPE

Jack Woodville London

Courage

"You men stand at ease." Colonel Henderson looked at his notepad, scribbled something, then looked back up at the pilot and door gunner standing in front of him in the LZ command post. "You say you saw civilians on the road? Is that right? About how many?"

"Eight to ten, Sir. And a water buffalo." Mr. Thompson, the pilot, a warrant officer, tried to unclench his jaw and release the grip in his hands. He had already broken his flight helmet and was afraid that if he didn't settle down he wouldn't make any sense.

"And then you landed? Is that right?" He wrote *landed* on his notepad, then looked up again. "Then what?"

Thompson's concern proved correct. He had poured out the story so fast that he got it out wrong. He took a deep breath and started over.

"No, Sir. What happened is that we were flying shoelaces over the road and saw the civilians, then we peeled off and saw some wounded, and we marked them with smoke."

Thompson closed his eyes and remembered. In his mind he again saw the people on the dirt road, as plainly as if he was back there. The village, a hundred yards to the west, had gone up in flames, all the thatched huts on fire. The only stone building in the hamlet, the one with the columns, had been knocked down by artillery fire. He had observed a soldier on the ground pointing a rifle down a well and another dumping rice into a sewer pit.

"Sir?" *click* went his headphones, as his crew chief got on the intercom. "What happened to those people on the road?" Andreotta meant the people who, not ten minutes before, had been running away.

Thompson had keyed his microphone to answer, then realized that the peasants now were sprawled all over the path. There were babies, children, women, very old men, the same ones, but now riddled with bullet holes. Even the water buffalo had been shot to death. He rolled the cyclic and pitched downward to swing the helicopter over the road. A wounded woman appeared on the far side of the trees and he lifted the nose to fly toward her.

"Drop smoke."

His other crewman dropped a green smoke canister near the woman.

"Dolphin One, this is Scout One," he spoke over his radio to a larger helicopter flying on top. "Need medevac dustoff. Girl on the grass."

Turn, climb, turn.

"What the hell?" *click*

Thompson knew that he was in the headquarters, reporting to the colonel, with his eyes closed, but his mind was still flying over the village, where he saw an infantry captain on the ground run up to the woman, green smoke drifting near her. The captain kicked her once, then lifted his rifle and put a bullet into her head.

Thompson felt himself shaking.

"We were hovering, Sir. Six, eight feet off the ground, maybe twenty feet away, watching him. He just shot her. She was already wounded. I'd called in a dustoff for her, and this guy shot her."

Colonel Henderson made a note on his pad. *Smoke*

Thompson then had put the helicopter into a short climb, pulled the cyclic, and circled back west of the village, where he saw the ditch. Heads. Legs. Arms. Bodies. The babies' faces were round, eyes wide, mouths twisted, most still being clutched by their dead mothers. Some of the bodies in the ditch were writhing.

"Shark One? This is Scout One." *click* "Relay to Command/ Control for me. It looks to me like there's an awful lot of unnecessary killing going on down there. Something ain't right about this. There's bodies everywhere."

"Shark One."

Thompson had pulled the collective and landed the scout helicopter in front of the ditch. A lieutenant on the ground approached; Thompson pushed his way past Andreotta to get out of the helicopter.

"What's going on here, Lieutenant?" he had shouted.

"This is my business."

"What is this? Who are these people?"

"Just following orders."

"Whose orders?"

"Just following."

"But these are human beings, unarmed civilians, Sir."

"Look, Thompson, this is my show. I'm in charge here. It ain't your concern."

"Yeah, great job."

"You better get back in that chopper and mind your own business."

"You ain't heard the last of this."

Thompson had backed away toward the glass canopy of the helicopter, keeping his eyes on the lieutenant and on the writhing ditch just beyond him. A sergeant stepped up to the ditch and fired into it. The bodies stopped writhing.

Ditch, the colonel noted. *That goddamned Barker,* he thought. *That dumb sonofabitch is flying around in the command / control chopper right on top of this goddamned mess.* He looked up at the pilot and his door gunner, a Spec 4 named Colburn. Thompson was in his flight suit, Colburn in his fatigues. They still had blood on their clothes, especially the sleeves. *My first day in charge of this fucked-up brigade and they start shooting people in a ditch.* He looked at the word again. *Ditch.*

"Did you get their names, Mr. Thompson?"

Thompson hadn't even tried to read their name tapes. The lieutenant had been shouting at him while cradling a machine gun across his chest. The soldier who had fired into the ditch was turned away from him. He had gotten into the helicopter and keyed the intercom.

"Did you see that?"

"Yessir."

"Hang on."

They had lifted off and circled back to the west.

More infantry, M-16s at the ready, was advancing toward a group of women and children who were running toward a bunker on the north side of the village. Thompson scooted just above the trees, turned the helicopter to face the platoon, and landed between it and the fleeing civilians.

"Dolphin One, this is Scout One. Come in." *click*

"Dolphin One."

"I'm down on the northeast corner. Do you see me?"

"20-20."

"Top cover."

He had said something to Andreotta and Colburn when he got out of the helicopter, but what it was just wouldn't come back into his memory. His two crewmen also stepped out and clutched their M-60s. The civilians made it to the bunker behind his helicopter and huddled. Thompson then had jogged forward to the platoon leader on the ground.

"Hey," he had yelled. The helicopter's main rotor whumped in the air at idle, *whump whump*, shaking the ground. "Hey, hold your fire. I'm going to try to get these people out of that bunker. Just hold your men here."

He hadn't known that lieutenant either. He should have asked their names, or made a point of looking at their tapes, anything.

"We can help you get 'em out, Mister. With a hand grenade."

"Just hold your men here. I think I can do better than that." Thompson had caught his breath, waiting to see if the platoon leader would indeed hold his men in place. The lieutenant jerked his head in a nonchalant direction, toward an NCO; his men relaxed in place. Some sat on the ground, others took out field rations and began to rip the cans open. Thompson then walked back to his helicopter.

"Stand here," he said to both Colburn and Andreotta. The crew chief and the door gunner stayed beside the glass canopy while the pilot reached into the console and pulled out his microphone.

"Dolphin One, this is Scout One." *click* "I'm holding in place on the ground. Can you land to evacuate about a dozen civilians? They're in a bunker right behind my chopper."

The larger helicopter didn't answer over the radio frequency. Instead, Thompson had felt its rotor wash come over him as Dolphin One set down. He turned back to his crew and said, "Cover me." He made eye contact, they understood, and Thompson ran to the bunker, then herded the terrified civilians toward Dolphin One, its doors off and rotor turning slowly.

Within three minutes all the women and babies and old men were on board.

"Sir!" Colonel Henderson raised his voice. "Thompson? You okay?" He snapped his fingers and Thompson jerked his consciousness back into the commander's office in the LZ. "You need some coffee or something? How long you been out there?"

"About 0700 this morning. We refueled a couple of times. One trip to the hospital, Sir. I'm all right. This is just...."

"How the hell did you guys get all that blood on you?"

Dolphin One had lifted off to take the civilians to a safer zone. Scout One had then lifted off to return for fuel. The flight path took it directly back over the ditch, where Andreotta had yelled at Thompson.

"Land, Sir! Hurry!" *click* "The ditch! Something's moving!"

The helicopter was a couple of feet off the ground and settling when Andreotta jumped from his seat and ran. Thompson and Colburn had watched him dig right into the bodies and pull a child out from under a shot-up corpse. The crew chief carried back a bloodied lump of baby, clothed in nothing but underwear, and climbed into the helicopter. They had delivered the child to a field hospital in the division rear area.

Quaing Ngai – hospital, the colonel wrote on his notepad. He looked out the window of his command post. My Lai wasn't more than two kilometers away, on the plain toward the Pinkville estuary. He gazed at the smoke rising from burned hooches and, he suspected, bodies. He had flown over the village himself after Barker ordered the cease fire, but he hadn't seen the numbers of bodies described by the pilot now standing in front of him.

"Trees, Sir. The ditch was right up against the trees. Unless your helicopter was low, west of the trees, and facing east it would have been hard to see them."

"So that's why I just saw the VC bodies on the road?"

"I don't know about VC, Sir. I just saw babies and women."

"Do you know anything about the VC count, Mr. Thompson? Or the weapons cache?" Lieutenant Colonel Barker had radioed a body count of one hundred twenty-eight dead VC and a bunch of weapons. It had been a good day, except that Colonel Henderson hadn't seen one hundred twenty-eight VC bodies either.

"Okay, Mr. Thompson. Thank you. Will you step outside a moment? You stay, Specialist."

Thompson saluted the new brigade commander and turned to leave. He, too, could see the smoke still rising in a plume above My Lai. A Chinook was landing on the pad just outside the command post. The Dolphins had flown back to Quaing Ngai. It seemed stark, and humid.

"At ease, Specialist. You were door gunner, is that right?" Henderson looked at Colburn, sized him up, saw a scared nineteen-year-old.

"Yes, Sir."

"That stuff Mr. Thompson was saying, about the bodies in the ditch and shooting that woman. Is that true?"

"Yes, Sir. I think there must have been more than fifty bodies in the ditch, Sir. Plus what we saw on the road."

Fifty to sixty in ditch, he wrote on the notepad, plus *road.*

"And that soldier shooting into the ditch?"

"I heard a shot, Sir, but my seat is at an angle to the pilot, so I didn't actually see the man shoot."

"And the dustoff for the civilians?"

"Yes, Sir. We landed. Mr. Thompson got out and stopped the men on the ground. We called in one of the Hueys and it took them off. Then we landed and picked up the baby and took it to the hospital. Then Mr. Thompson said we had to come report this."

Henderson thought for a moment, then called out through the door for Thompson to come back inside.

"Men, thank you for reporting this. I'll look into it. That's all." He stiffened and waited for them to salute. They saluted. "And men? I'll tell you what. It took a lot of courage for you to come in and report this. A lot of courage. Thanks."

"You're welcome, Sir."

Hope

Henderson waited until the pilot and the door gunner left his command post. He looked out his window and watched them walk back to the scout helicopter, wondering if they were in any shape to fly. He heard sounds on the other side of the partition, a duty clerk typing away, his XO talking to a logistics officer about resupply, some chatter about intelligence reports. He closed his door, walked back to the desk, and picked up his notepad.

He tore his notes into tiny pieces, then lit them with his Zippo lighter. They burned to ashes. He crushed the ashes in his hand.

Hope, he thought. *I hope to God this never gets out.*

Then he called the duty clerk in. It was time to bring Lieutenant Colonel Barker into the CP so that they could write up the VC body count.

Author's Note: Thompson, Colburn, and Andreotta were awarded the Distinguished Flying Cross for their heroic work at My Lai. Andreotta was killed by a sniper less than a month later. Thompson and Colburn were broken up as a crew shortly afterward. Lieutenant Colonel Barker died in a mid-air collision in Vietnam. Hugh Thompson died in 2006, with Larry Colburn at his side. Because of the deaths and because of the destruction of Colonel Henderson's notes, some of the dialogue is fictionalized although drawn entirely from Thompson's,

Colburn's, and Henderson's testimony of the events at Colonel Henderson's, Captain Medina's, and Lieutenant Calley's trials and on the congressional report of the My Lai investigation.

Jack Woodville London

Jack Woodville London is an author in Austin, Texas. He studied creative writing at Oxford University and the Academy of Fiction, St. Céré, France. His articles, reviews, and historical commentaries have been published in *On Patrol* (journal of the USO military service organization), *Stars and Stripes*, *Dispatches*, (journal of the Military Writers Society of America), *The Huffington Post*, *Austin American Statesman*, and civilian and military newspapers throughout the United States and Europe. He was honored as Author of the Year (2011-2012) by Military Writers Society of America and is a member of and on the Awards Committee of the Center for Fiction, New York City.

His first two novels, *Virginia's War* and *Engaged in War*, won awards in contests ranging from Best Novel of the South, Romantic Novels with a Twist, and Historical Fiction, Silver Medal in the London (England) Literary Festival, and overall winner, Indie Excellence Award (2013). His fiction work in progress will complete that series; its working title is *Children of a Good War*. His third book, *A Novel Approach*, released in September 2014, is a short and lighthearted work on the craft and conventions of writing designed to help writers who are setting out on the path to writing their first book. It won the eLit 2015 gold medal for books on the craft of writing.

48

A TALE OF TWO WARS

Earl Dusty Trimmer

While this is not a tale of two cities by Dickens, it is a tale about two wars fought by Vietnam War era's veterans. It was the best of times; it was the worst of times. It was the age of judgment; it was the age of the unthinkable. It was the epoch of disbelief; it was the epoch of doubt. It was the season of night; it was the season of day. It was the spring of hope; it was the winter of our disillusionment. We had everything before us. And we were left with almost nothing. We were all going directly to heaven. We were all going through hell first.

In short, the Vietnam era was so far removed from the present that many of its survivors cannot help but remember it for good and for evil as an era that compared with no other before, or so far, after. As a result of our long imprisonment, many of today's survivors from the Vietnam War suffer from a form of psychosis, an obsession with making our story right, telling it over and again until it is accepted or at least heard. Enter—*A Tale of Two Wars*.

The War Over There

My war over there began in March 1968, right at the end of one Tet Offensive in February and the very beginning of another one in May. My new family and I were initiated instantly in the cruelest manner, jumping right into face-to-face combat situations. At the outset of our vacation in Vietnam, our twenty-seven man platoon of Bravo Company 3rd 22nd of the 25th Infantry Division was pushed to our limits with a record eighty-eight consecutive days in the boonies—no showers, no hot meals, infrequent mail delivery by helicopter, no beds, no shelter, period—as the living conditions were too abysmal for words to describe.

Search and destroy by day and seek and ambush by night—same routine 24/7 and every so often we might sneak in two hours of shut-eye. One brother after another fell. Most we never saw again. Soon our original twenty-seven of the 1st Platoon were minus ten. I saw one point man after another go down in the first couple of weeks, usually new guys who lasted a couple of weeks, so I volunteered—actually demanded to become a permanent point man. We never walked into an ambush again for ten weeks until June 15, 1968. That day we would lose half of the original twenty-seven and a couple of the new guys as well. I spotted the Viet Cong ambush in time so that all of those behind me in our squad hit the ground a couple seconds before the enemy fire began. But the second squad didn't get those two seconds and their entire file was mowed down. I did take a round through my helmet, grazing my head, but I would live for another day. The remainder of that day requires a long story by itself to give it justice. Heroes were born that day.

A couple weeks later and a couple more brothers were re-placed. We had been sent to aid a sister company that was under attack near Trang Bang. I was on top of an armored personnel carrier (APC) when it was rocked by a rocket-propelled grenade (RPG), knocking me from the APC, landing on my head and knocked unconscious. A concussion was likely, but I didn't feel it. I was out. They medivac'd me with the other wounded to be attended to at a small clinic at our base camp called Dau Tieng, which wasn't much more than a glorified outpost.

It was July 3, 1968 and I was scheduled to be examined the next morning on July 4. The exam was unexpectedly and rudely interrupted.

In the early hours of July 4, Dau Tieng came under attack. Before this battle had ended, the assault on Dau Tieng would rank as the largest attack of the small base camp's history. Over four hundred rockets and mortars were sent into Dau Tieng that morning before daylight. The noise was deafening. The base camp was overrun, but we would prevail and I would live to fight another day. I was never treated for the head injury, plus I had taken minor shrapnel wounds to my knee and foot, which took a few stitches and band-aids and I was sent back to the field with my war buddies. That was how a few days went of my war experience in-country, South Vietnam.

The War Over Here

The Vietnam War continues to agonize many of us to this day and it seems so unfair. We paid our dues. We did a full year's tour in hell and now we are cursed with the memories and illnesses of that war for the rest of our lives. Is there any hope, I often wonder? Are Vietnam War veterans condemned property? We never gave up over there, and by God, I'm not going to give up back here. So I wrote a book and named it—what else—*Condemned Property?*

In writing my story, I experienced a desperately needed cathartic effect. Never being shy about speaking out about our wars, both with an enemy in Vietnam and a government cursed with indifference afterwards, I've written about my own battles with post traumatic stress disorder, other chronic medical issues, and bizarre dances with a bureaucracy that denies, delays, denies, and denies. My story is a personal account of an anguishing experience shared by many and brought back home by too many who have been unable to leave the profane violence experienced in the fields and jungles of Vietnam.

America needs to know that Vietnam War veterans' love for our country still runs deep. America also needs to understand what Vietnam War veterans have had to overcome since coming home. We survivors have faced and overcome many life-threatening and life-altering challenges, and we still face several difficult life events such as retirement, disability, and a staggering ongoing premature loss of lives of those who served with us.

My message is the summation of lives lived with honor: that the men and women who have borne much ask for little more than an old-fashioned handshake, a pat on their backs, a simple "attaboy," and a little respect for their courage.

We are no longer those lost and unwanted kids of the 1960s and 1970s. Today we have hope and I am proud to say that Vietnam War era veterans are one of America's greatest generations.

Earl Dusty Trimmer

Earl Dusty Trimmer has been a successful marketing professional for over forty years, representing several mega publishing companies. Forced into retirement due to a disabling illness associated with his heavy exposure to Agent Orange in the Vietnam War, he has tried to fill that void in his life as an author.

He was drafted into the U.S. Army in October 1967, declining an opportunity to attend Officers Candidate School (OCS), and electing instead to fulfill his obligation to America as a combat infantryman in Vietnam. Some of his military honors include the Combat Infantry Badge, Bronze Star for Valor, Purple Heart, Army Commendation Medal, and the Vietnam Cross of Gallantry. Discharged with the rank of Specialist E-5, he served one year in the U.S. National Guard as a sergeant.

Trimmer recalls his struggles to convert almost overnight from a shy civilian to a hardened combat specialist, thrust into one of the most hazardous combat areas of operation during the Tet year of 1968. Life, as he knew it, was abruptly turned upside down. His first two books, *Condemned Property?* and *Payback Time!* are about the brave American soldiers he served with in Vietnam. They were every bit as courageous and patriotic as all other American soldiers who risked their lives or died in previous wars. *Condemned Property?* was an MWSA finalist in the memoir category and the Army Heritage Center Foundation hailed it for honoring servicemen and women, preserving their stories, and educating future generations about their selfless service.

The Medal of Honor
It in Afghanistan and Iraq
Gold Medal Award
John D. Gresham
ER'S AWARD

49

REQUIEM FOR BRAVO 6

Dwight Jon Zimmerman

STORY: DWIGHT JON ZIMMERMAN / ART: JUAN CARLOS ABRALDES RENDO

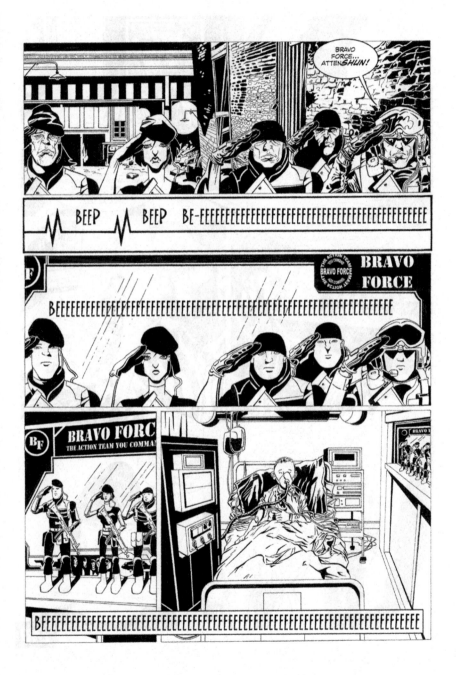

Dwight Jon Zimmerman

Dwight Jon Zimmerman is a best-selling and award-winning author, radio show host, and television and movie producer, as well as the current president of Military Writers Society of America (MWSA). He began his career at Marvel Comics, and has written stories about most of its famous characters. He has written more than a dozen books and over 300 articles on military history.

His latest works include the graphic biography *Steve McQueen: Full-Throttle Cool* (July 2015) and the *Smithsonian National Air and Space Museum Photographic Card Deck: 100 Treasures from the World's Largest Collection of Aircraft and Spacecraft* (September 2015). In 2012, Zimmerman coauthored the New York Times best-selling book, *Lincoln's Last Days*, a young adult adaptation of Bill O'Reilly's *Killing Lincoln*.

Zimmerman is the coauthor, with John D. Gresham, of *Uncommon Valor: The Medal of Honor and the Six Warriors Who Earned It in Afghanistan and Iraq*, which received the MWSA Founder's Award for 2010.

Zimmerman was the co-executive producer of the Military Channel miniseries, *First Command*, based on his book of the same name. It won the 2005 Aurora Platinum Best of Show Award for Historical Programming.

Zimmerman has lectured at the U.S. Military Academy at West Point and the Naval War College, and has appeared on the Fox News programs, DEFCON-3 and America's News HQ. He lives in Brooklyn, New York, with his wife Joëlle.